50 FAVORITE HIKES

FLAGSTAFF & SEDONA

"Not all those who wander are lost."
J.R.R. Tolkien

PRINTED ON RECYCLED PAPER WITH 100% BLOOD, SWEAT & VEGETABLE INK.

RATINGS

FOR COMPARISON'S SAKE, ALL HIKES WERE RATED BY ME, A SEEDY BUT SINCERE MIDDLE AGE MALE IN REASONABLE PHYSICAL CONDITION IF OTHERWISE UNENCUMBERED BY THE THOUGHT PROCESS.

EASY: Some hills with nothing too steep or too long. A stroll in the park. A beginner hike. A weenie walk.

MODERATE: Your brow may drip. Your head may pound. Your heart may even hammer. However, you will not die. Interesting terrain with some effort required.

DIFFICULT: Real effort. Includes some climbing and distance. Like straight espresso . . . if you don't know what it is, you don't want it. Not for the feeble.

WARNING

(IT AIN'T RAY'S FAULT!)

This book is no substitute for topo maps, route finding skill, compass, good judgement, sense of humor, manners or cognitive thought. I've done my level best. I am not responsible for sun, wind, rain, flash flood, lightning, wild beasts, sign changes, slippery slopes, puddles, detours, falls, pulled muscles, blisters or any other misfortune that may get your knicks in a twist.

Know that it is your job to be familiar with route, water supply, mind set, companions, undies, acts of God, lions, tigers, bears and every other darn thing.

Furthermore, you hereby release me, my heirs and representatives from mistakes, getting lost, hurt, scared or tired. And last but not least, it is OK to be weak of physique or lame of brain, but if you be thin of grin, PLEASE STAY SAFE AT HOME!

CLOTHING: Sturdy, lightweight hiking shoes and good socks for most trails. Sports sandals (Tevas) for creeks. A hat and shades for sun. A scarf. Layers of clothing for cooler days. I use a t-shirt, sweatshirt, fleece jacket and a Gore-Tex outer shell. Put on or peel off as the day dictates.

FOOD & WATER: A little food and a lot of water. Fruit, energy bars and sandwiches work great. Candy bars suck. Drink at least 1 quart of water for every 5 miles plus 1 quart for every 1000 feet of elevation gain. Hydrate frequently.

OTHER STUFF: A small, comfy pack. Swiss army knife. Tweezers for thorns. Glasses, compass, lighter, bug repellent, aspirin, #15 sunscreen, TP, ziploc baggies and moleskin for blisters. A map and a pal (very important!). Tiny camera and/or binocs may add to enjoyment.

IF YOU DESIRE RESPECT, YOU MUST GIVE SAME.

Death to micro-trash! Leave the environment better than you found it so all may enjoy. Butts, matches, peels, cores, crumbs, dog doo, used TP, wrappers, small bits of found glass, etc. all go in that baggie you brought. Leave NOTHING! ZIP! ZERO! Do a good deed, adopt some trash.

Respect the ancients. Do not touch petroglyphs or pictographs. Over time, oils from many hands ruin the art. Do not disturb ruins or pick up artifacts. No stealing. You may go to jail and/or acquire a curse. No joke!

Respect the trail. Your new trail or shortcut speeds erosion and kills fragile desert vegetation. Stay on the trail. No fires. No smoking. No yelling. No shooting. No bad stuff. Just do the right thing and you'll have no worries.

ABINEAU & BEAR JAW TRAILS

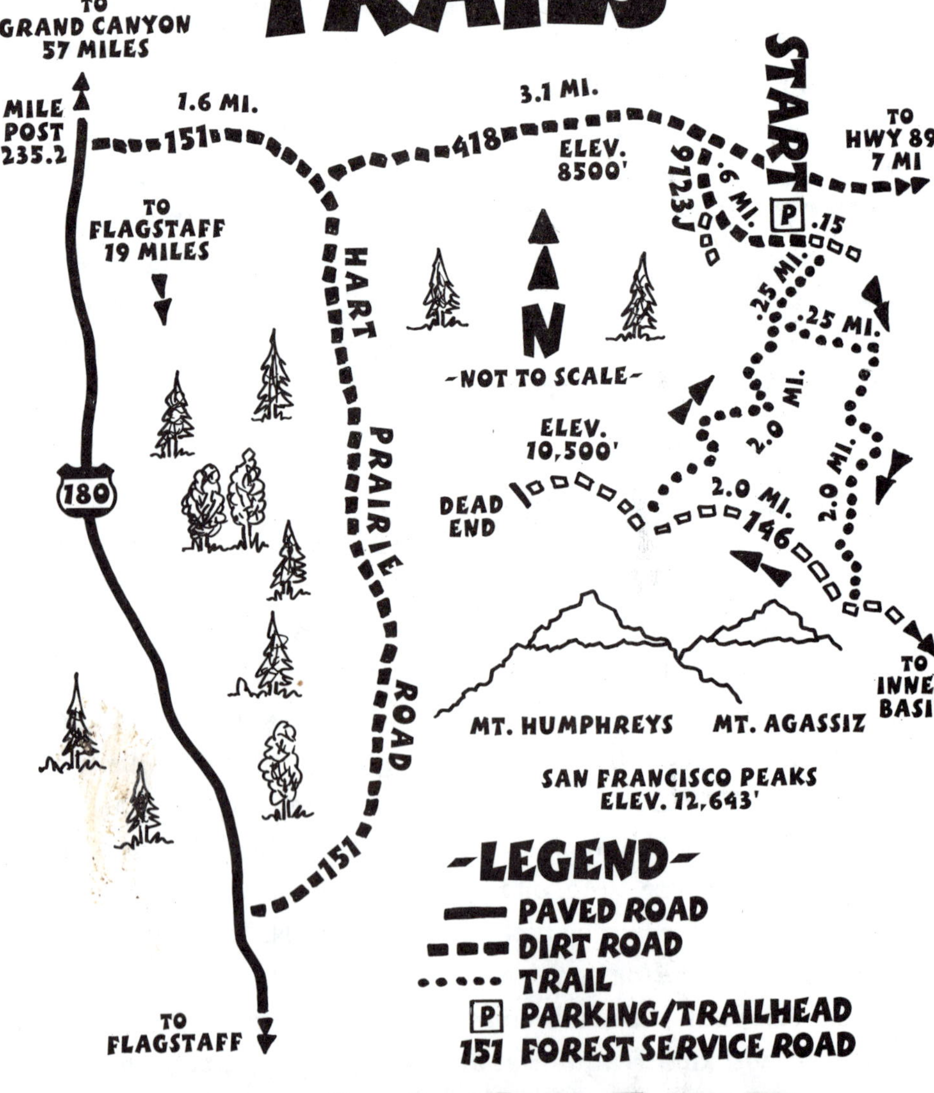

FLAGSTAFF

RAY

ABINEAU/BEAR JAW TRAILS

SCENIC LOOP NORTH OF THE PEAKS

DISTANCE: 7.1 MILES
TIME: 4 to 5 HOURS
EFFORT: HARD
TYPE: LOOP
ROUTE FINDING: EASY
SEASON: MAY to NOV

CONTOUR PROFILE

DESCRIPTION: This high altitude loop on the north side of the San Francisco Peaks ascends Bear Jaw Trail through storybook stands of towering conifer and aspen. You'll break out of the trees above timberline to breathe in views expanding to The Grand Canyon's North Rim 90 miles distant. Take notice of the power of nature when an avalance scoured this canyon just a few years ago. Giant old growth trees in its path were swept away like toothpicks while others just inches away were spared. Glad I wasn't here that winter day.

Cool, high altitude Abineau-Bear Jaw Trails are well suited to desert refugees seeking respite from Arizona's summer oven. In the fall, flowers and stands of aspen splash the slopes crimson and gold. If you're quiet and early, shy black bear, deer and elk are not uncommon. Birdsong fills the air.

Be prepared for sun or heavy cold summer rain even if the sky is clear when you begin. Up here, fleecy clouds quickly boil black. I got caught out in it one fine summer day and was really happy to see my truck at the end. Wear a hat. Carry food and water. Can be done as a loop or a shorter simple up and down.

DIRECTIONS: Take highway 180 north 19 miles out of Flagstaff heading toward Grand Canyon. At milepost 235.2 turn right onto gravel forest road 151. After 1.6 miles, bear left onto 418 for 3.1 miles then a final right onto 9123J 0.6 miles to the trailhead parking area. All roads are smooth and well marked.

BUFFALO PARK

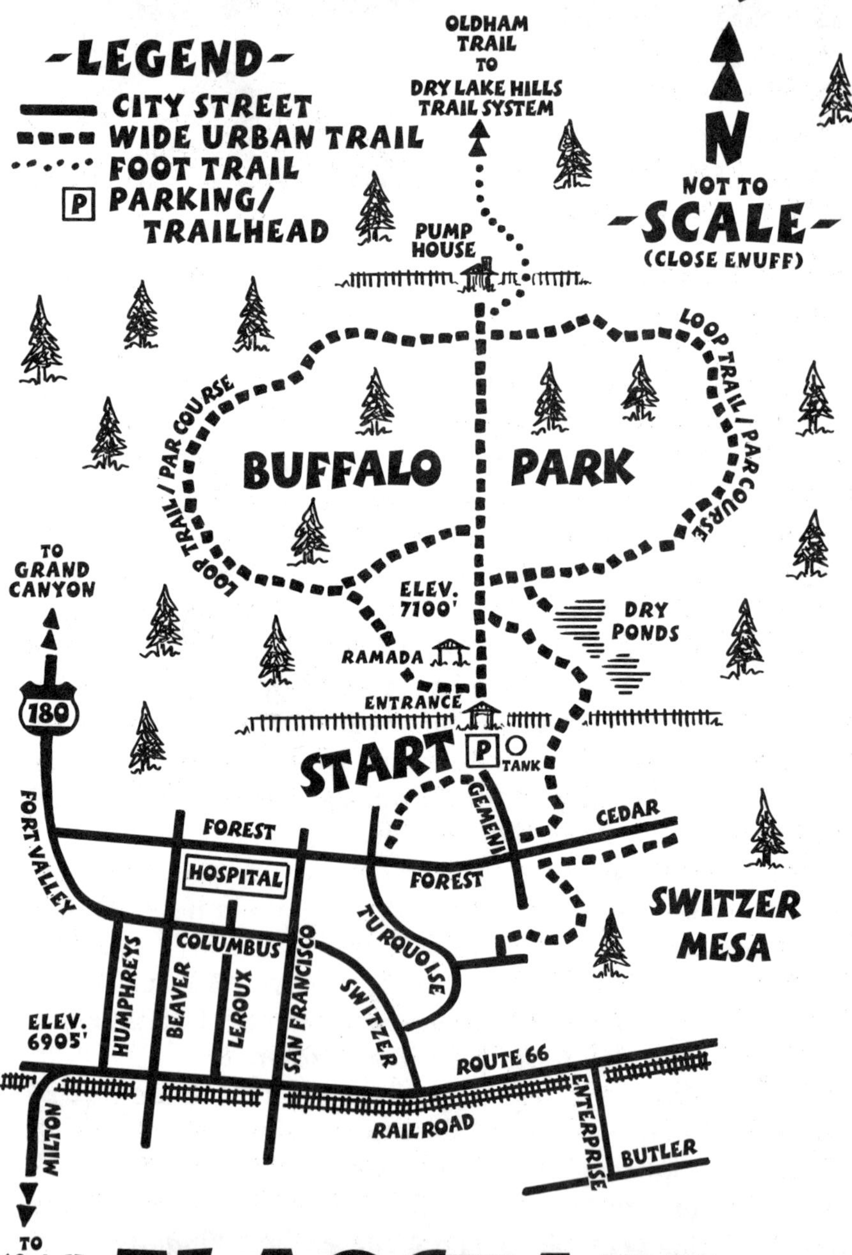

FLAGSTAFF

BUFFALO PARK
EASY LOOP THROUGH URBAN PARK

DISTANCE: 2.0 MILES
TIME: 0.5 to 1 HOUR
EFFORT: NO SWEAT
TYPE: SHORT LOOP
FIND ROUTE: EASY
SEASON: ALL YEAR

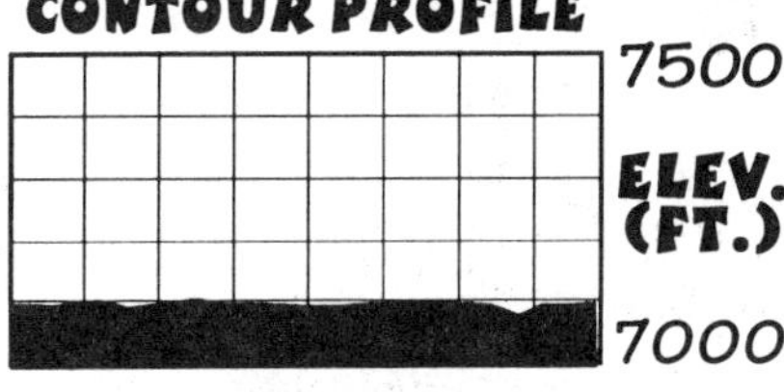

DESCRIPTION: A wonderfully wild Flagstaff city park offers quick, convenient and easy exercise opportunity for walkers, bikers, joggers, X-C skiers and their pets. Located atop a sparsely treed mesa 200 ft. above the bustling city, a flat, smooth, easy 2-mile loop containing a moderate par course meanders through an open field bisected by a dirt service road.

Constructed in the 1960s, this failed wild animal park venture is a godsend to the people of Flagstaff hungry for open space inside city limits. Flag voters have often wisely rejected roads in or near the park. The entrance shelter and stone buffalo buffalo statue are all that remain of the theme park pipe dream, but the park itself stands as a symbol of all that is great about this mountain town.

Sensational views of Mt. Elden's gnarled, boulder strewn face and The San Francisco Peaks high above have long provided a backdrop for relaxing walks, school outdoor events, lunch hour runs, evening strolls, weddings and other activities. Long live The Buffalo!

DIRECTIONS: From downtown Flagstaff, head north on N. San Francisco St. 1.2 miles to Forest Ave. Turn right and go up the hill to Gemini. Turn left and park in the lot. Take your picture atop the Buffalo.

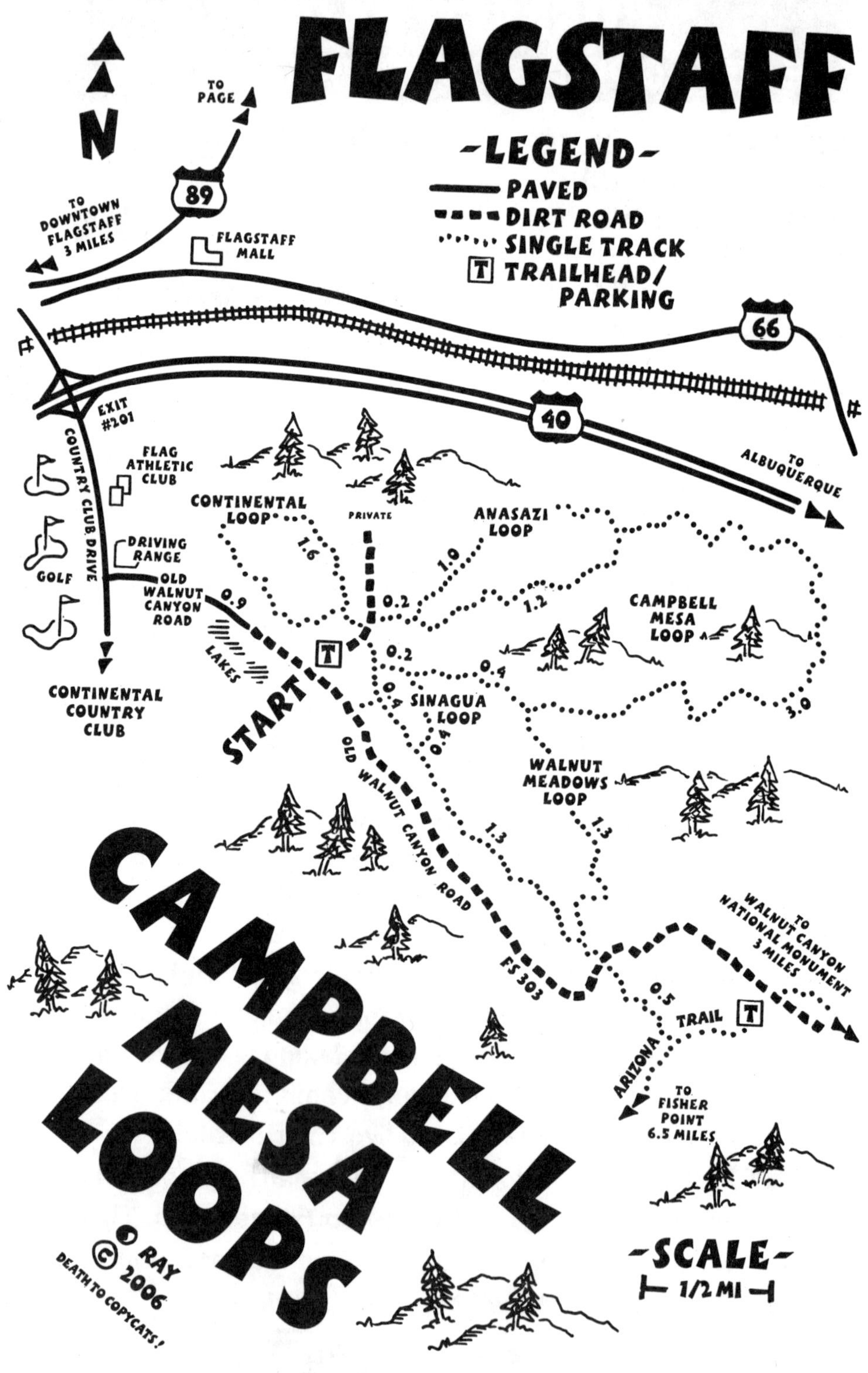
FLAGSTAFF
N
TO PAGE
89
TO DOWNTOWN FLAGSTAFF 3 MILES
FLAGSTAFF MALL
-LEGEND-
PAVED
DIRT ROAD
SINGLE TRACK
TRAILHEAD/ PARKING
66
40
EXIT #201
COUNTRY CLUB DRIVE
FLAG ATHLETIC CLUB
GOLF
DRIVING RANGE
OLD WALNUT CANYON ROAD
0.9
LAKES
CONTINENTAL COUNTRY CLUB
TO ALBUQUERQUE
CONTINENTAL LOOP
1.6
PRIVATE
ANASAZI LOOP
1.0
0.2
1.2
CAMPBELL MESA LOOP
0.2
0.4
0.4
SINAGUA LOOP
0.4
3.0
START
OLD WALNUT CANYON ROAD
WALNUT MEADOWS LOOP
1.3
1.3
FS 303
TO WALNUT CANYON NATIONAL MONUMENT 3 MILES
0.5
TRAIL
ARIZONA
TO FISHER POINT 6.5 MILES
CAMPBELL MESA LOOPS
© RAY 2006
DEATH TO COPYCATS!
-SCALE-
1/2 MI

CAMPBELL MESA TRAILS
EASY LOOP TRAILS, GREAT WILDFLOWERS

DISTANCE: 1 TO 9 MILES
TIME: 1 TO 3 HOURS
EFFORT: EASY TO MEDIUM
TYPE: FIVE LOOP TRAILS
FIND ROUTE: ALL SIGNED
SEASON: APR to NOV

CONTOUR PROFILE

DESCRIPTION: Great for a family outing. Like spokes from a wheel, these easy loops radiate out from a central trailhead hub located up a dirt road about 100 meters beyond the parking lot gate.

The short Continental Loop is a good start to see how you like the area. An easy climb to start then the loop rolls around and back down to where you began in only 1.6 miles. You have views of town and Mt. Elden and every turn is well marked.

You can see from the map that there are four other gently rolling, smooth, longer loops, all well marked. The area is very uncrowded and lovely. The forest is open and scattered with oak, juniper, pinon and ponderosa pine. During and after summer monsoon rain, the mesa is ablaze with wildflowers and carpeted with native grasses. With all the signs, you can't get lost if you just avoid the spur that directs you onto The Arizona Trail. See map.

DIRECTIONS: Easy to find near Continental Country Club in East Flagstaff. From I-40, take CCC/Page Exit #201. Head south 0.9 miles to Old Walnut Canyon Road. Take a LEFT and go another 0.9 miles to the parking lot on the LEFT. OR from downtown flagstaff, take Route 66 EAST until you see the sign for Continental Country Club. Bear RIGHT over the overpass and follow the map.

DRY LAKE HILLS

FLAGSTAFF

DRY LAKE HILLS
SCENIC DRY LAKE AND GREAT VIEW

DISTANCE: 5 MILES
TIME: 2 to 3 HOURS
EFFORT: MODERATE
TYPE: OUT & BACK
FIND ROUTE: FAIRLY EASY
SEASON: APR to NOV

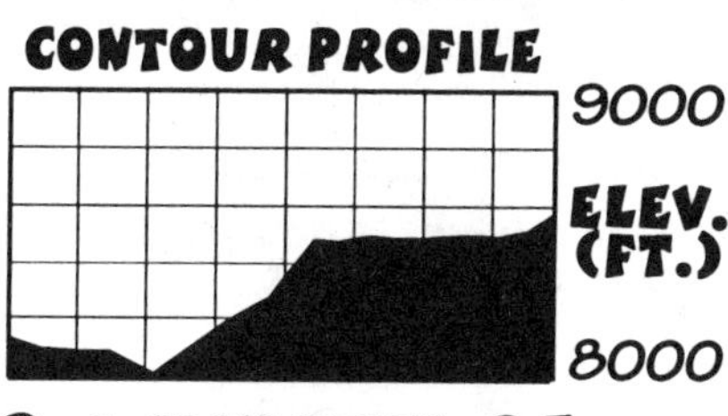

FLAGSTAFF

DESCRIPTION: From historic downtown Flagstaff look due north toward The San Francisco Peaks. In front of The Peaks set a group of richly forested hills. Invisible from town, but set down in between these hills is a lovely green, grassy dry lakebed of wildflowers filled with water only during spring snowmelt. Aspen, fir, pine and spruce blanket the surrounding hills. Elk, deer, bear and many bird species inhabit this fine mixed forest. I accidently set a flock of 50 or so wild turkey hens and young'uns ascramble here early one morning. A secret rock outcrop (see map) offers a great settin' spot, view of Flagstaff and good goal for this hike.

DIRECTIONS: Go north out of Flag on Highway 180 for 2 miles to milepost 218.6. Turn right onto Schultz Pass Rd. Continue as it turns dirt after 0.7 miles, careful not to go up Elden Lookout Road. Go another 4.5 miles the signed Sunset Trail parking area. Head out of the parking area on a dirt road which leads to the Loop Trail. Follow the map until you reach a small fenced-in pond and a big open meadow, the first of the dry lakes. Bear RIGHT at the pond. Out at the end of the lake, the trail splits again. LEFT takes you to a great Flagstaff view. RIGHT leads out to a further dry lake and view. In fall, if you're real quiet and early, you'll likely see elk and turkey or at least find your peace among the wildflowers and shimmering gold aspen.

FATMAN'S LOOP

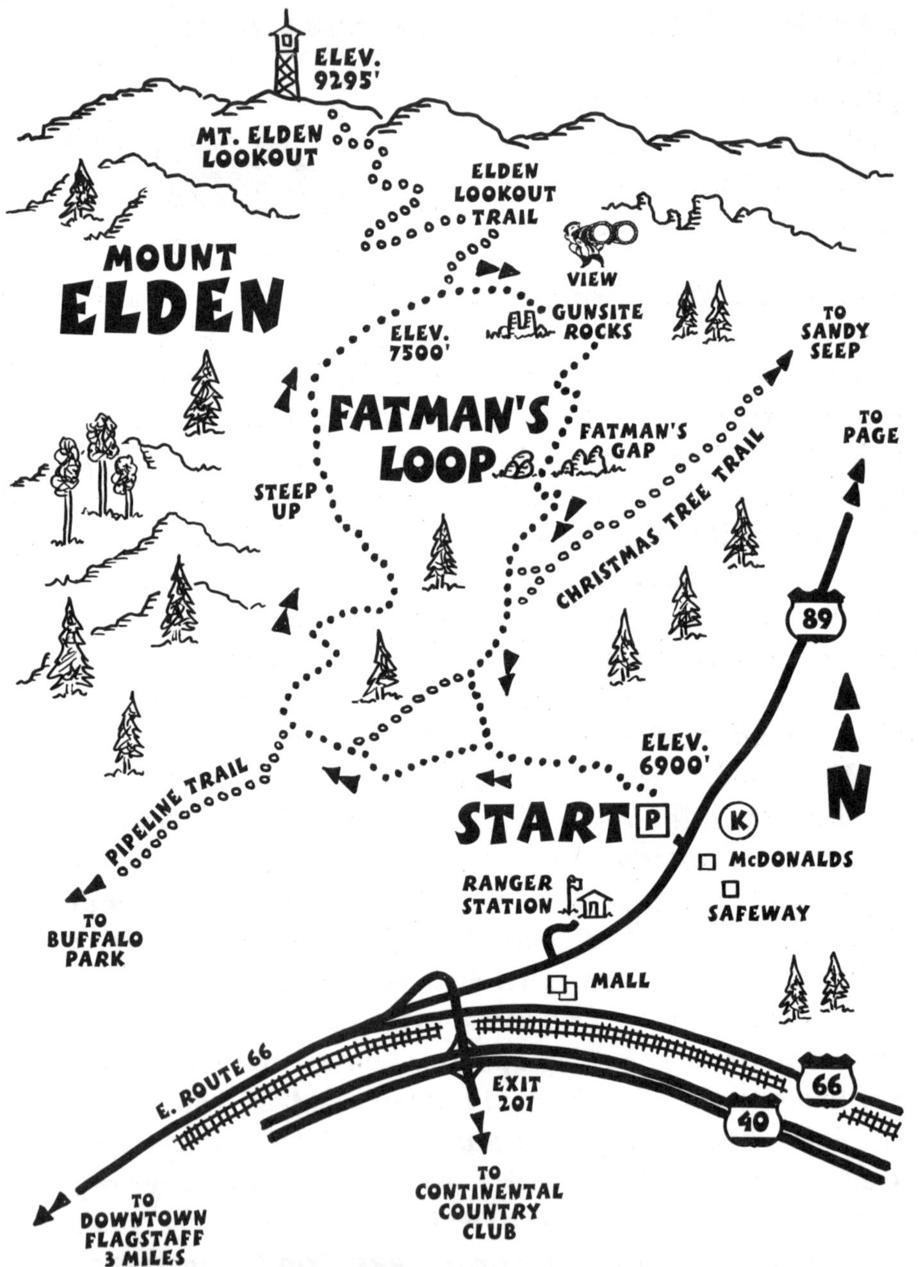

FLAGSTAFF

FATMAN'S LOOP
SHORT, STEEP & SCENIC TRAIL ON ELDEN

DISTANCE: 2 MILES
TIME: 1 to 1.5 HOURS
EFFORT: SHORT & STEEP
TYPE: LOOP
FIND ROUTE: EASY
SEASON: MAR TO DEC

DESCRIPTION: OK Tubby, I apologize for the name, but really, any male under 4 foot abeam can pass the test of Fat Man's Gap. Dr. Ray *promises* this short, steep loop at the base of Mt. Elden's sunny eastern slope will provide wicked good work and reduce the girth of any person able and willing to walk the walk.

The climb begins gradually for the first short bit then climbs steeply to the halfway mark at the junction with Mt. Elden Lookout Trail. After that, it's a cruise down the mountain, zipping past the Gunsite Rocks and down, down the narrow single track through a fatman's squeeze between the boulders. After a another short and nearly flat stretch, you're back at the trailhead. Whew! Do the whole thing 7 times more with a 30 lb. pack and you're ready to hike The Grand Canyon.

Fatman's Loop Trail passes through a diverse forest of oak, pinon, ponderosa pine, fir, broadleaf yucca and a few huge, fabulously gnarled alligator bark juniper. Fatman's is fairly crowded on weekends and deserted weekdays. Also, Fatman's gets sunny eastern exposure, so it can usually be hiked all winter.

DIRECTIONS: From downtown Flagstaff go 3 miles east on main drag Route 66 through East Flag. Continue toward Page on Highway 89. Mt. Elden Trailhead and Fatman's Loop are on the left just past McDonald's.

FISHER POINT (VIA SANDY'S CANYON)

FLAGSTAFF

FISHER POINT
OUT & BACK TRAIL TO CAVE & VIEW

DISTANCE: 5.8 MILES
TIME: 3 TO 4 HOURS
EFFORT: STRENUOUS
TYPE: OUT & BACK
FIND ROUTE: EASY
SEASON: APR to NOV

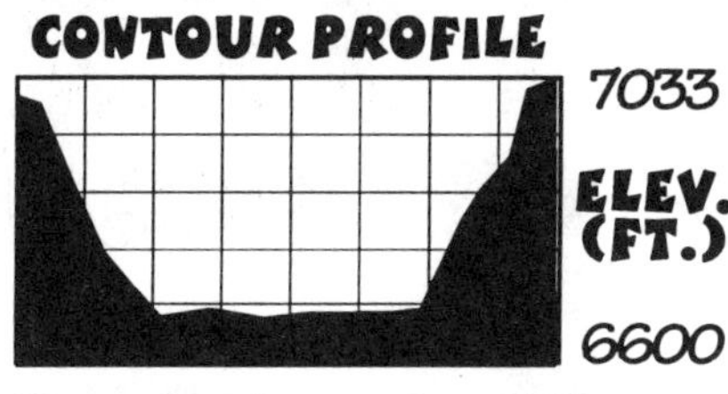

DESCRIPTION: Fisher Point sits atop a beautiful weather sculpted sandstone cliff 433 vertical feet above the mouth of Walnut Canyon. Get there via Sandy's Canyon Trail through a silent, heavily wooded canyon after descending from Lake Mary Road at a popular Flagstaff outdoor rock gym known as The Pit.

The well signed first mile follows along the canyon rim with views of The Pit and The Peaks then drops sharply and continues through a rocky wash to where it joins the Arizona Trail. The path smoothes out and after 0.9 miles you arrive for your first peek at Fisher Point. There is a large cave at the base. To your right is the entrance to Walnut Canyon, a beautiful place to explore . . . more caves, wildlife and cliff-dweller ruins.

Now look at the map and look around for the sign that leads you up that final mile via easy switchbacks to Fisher Point, a great lunch spot and bird's eye view of the canyon below.

DIRECTIONS: Find that cosmic spot in Flag where HWY 89A, I-40, I-17 and Lake Mary Road all collide near Wal-Mart. Go south on Lake Mary Road 5.6 miles just a little past the 2nd cattleguard and the Flagstaff city limit sign at milepost 338.4. Park in the lot.

GERONIMO SPRING (SYCAMORE CANYON)

FLAGSTAFF

GERONIMO SPRING
STEEP DROP INTO SYCAMORE CANYON

DISTANCE: 4 MILES
TIME: 3 TO 4 HOURS
EFFORT: SHORT & TOUGH
TYPE: DOWN & UP
FIND ROUTE: EASY
SEASON: MAR to NOV

FLAGSTAFF

DESCRIPTION: Hike-o-licious! If you like to hike, you have died and gone to heaven. It's a short, steep trail through a big-tree enchanted forest off the rim to the bottom of a pristine wilderness canyon. Flowers of every hue. Orange, blue and green dragonflies, lizards and horned toads, butterflies and birdsong, deer and elk . . . and water. Kelsey and Babe's Hole Springs punctuate the hike down plus Geronimo at the bottom. Big secret pools for swimming in the early spring.

The trail dives off the rim to Kelsey Spring in 0.5 miles then 0.75 miles down to Babe's Hole Spring. Just after Babe's Hole, the trail splits. Take the signed RIGHT fork toward Little LO Trail#6 and do the final way steep 0.75 mile descent to Geronimo Spring. Explore the canyon floor. Drink water then suck it up for the hike out.

DIRECTIONS: Head west out of Flagstaff 2 miles on Route 66 WEST. Turn LEFT onto Woody Mountain Road. Go 14.2 miles on this good dirt road. Turn RIGHT on FS538 and go another 5.5 miles to FS538E and turn right. From here follow the signs and the map to "Kelsey Spring Trail". The road gets rough as heck at the end, so you might want to walk the final half mile or so to the well marked trailhead. Worth the effort!

"When you come to a fork in the road, take it."
-*Yogi Berra*

SAN FRANCISCO PEAKS

HUMPHREYS PEAK TRAIL

FLAGSTAFF

HUMPHREYS PEAK TRAIL

HARD CLIMB TO THE TOP OF ARIZONA

DISTANCE: 9.6 MILES
TIME: 5 to 6 HOURS
EFFORT: DARN HARD
TYPE: OUT & BACK
FIND ROUTE: EASY
SEASON: MAY to OCT

FLAGSTAFF

DESCRIPTION: On this day you will get higher than a hippie in a helicopter. You'll stand above all others in the land of AZ. Ruler of all you survey. Well, let's not get carried away, but you will ascend to the top of Humphreys Peak, highest of the San Francisco Peaks and highest in Arizona at 12,633 ft. It's up there!

Plan for an all day outing. Bring food and water as well as protective clothing. If it begins to cloud up, it is time to bail. You would not be the first nor the last to be blown to kingdom come by a lightning bolt at this elevation. Talk about your bad hair day!

Beginning from the Snowbowl parking area, you cross an open grassy meadow then climb through a dark, dense forest of conifer and aspen to timberline at 10,500 ft. A barren rocky saddle is ahead just above at 11.,800. Once in the saddle the trail splits. You bear LEFT and continue up, up, up over a series of heart breaking false summits until you finally peak out.

For the respiratorily challenged, The AZ Snowbowl offers a summer chairlift skyride up neighboring Agassiz Peak for the view.

DIRECTIONS: North out of Flag 7 miles on Highway 180 to milepost 223. Go right onto Snow Bowl Road for 6.5 miles then turn left to the end of the parking area just below the lodge. Good spot for apres hike brews and snackage!

INNER BASIN (ASPENS & FALL COLORS)

FLAGSTAFF

INNER BASIN

ASPEN STROLL UP TO PEAKS VIEW

DISTANCE: 4 MILES
TIME: 2 HOURS
EFFORT: IT'S UPHILL
TYPE: OUT & BACK
FIND ROUTE: EASY
SEASON: MAY to OCT

DESCRIPTION: The essential autumn leaf looker. A great family hike to have a high altitude look at the Inner Basin of the San Francisco Peaks, an extinct volcano. The basin may have been formed when the volcano's magma chamber collapsed into itself or when the side of the mountain blew out sideways a la Mt. St. Helens. In any event, those days are long gone and most folks just come to look at The Peaks and the fall colors. XC skiers love it up here in winter when the trees are bare and 10 feet of snow buries the land.

The dirt road up to Lockett Meadow is steep in a couple of spots, but is very do-able with a car. Once in Locket Meadow, the trailhead is easy to find and the trail well worn leading up through a mixed forest of conifer and stands of shimmering aspen to a group of cabins. From there, continue straight ahead and up to The IB for those superb peak views. You might try another route down aspen covered backcountry road FS 146 (see map) for your return to Lockett Meadow.

DIRECTIONS: From downtown Flag head east on Route 66 through east Flag. Continue as it becomes HWY 89 heading toward Page. Go 12 miles to milepost 430.4 opposite Sunset Crater Road. Turn left here and follow the signs up Lockett Meadow Road.

KACHINA TRAIL

FLAGSTAFF

KACHINA TRAIL

FAIRLY EASY PEAKS HIKE WITH VIEWS

DISTANCE: 5 MILES
TIME: 2.5 TO 3 HOURS
EFFORT: MODERATE
TYPE: POINT TO POINT
FIND ROUTE: EASY
SEASON: MAR to NOV

FLAGSTAFF

DESCRIPTION: My heart sank to my knees as flames raced through the trees. Another favorite trail up in smoke thanks to a careless human, but it's not as bad as I first thought. The 2001 Leroux Fire only toasted a half mile stretch in the middle of the 6-mile trail. Crews have worked magic, hand tools and sweat to make this bit not only hikeable, but an opportunity to watch the forces of nature return the forest to health.

This is one trail on The San Francisco Peaks that doesn't head for the top. Kachina cuts *across* the slope of the 12,633 ft. Kachina Peaks Wilderness. It's easy hiking for most everyone as Kachina Trail mixes stands of aspen and conifer with meadows carpeted with wildflowers. In fall, aspen go gold and red as they bare their bones for winter in the high country. When the trail breaks out of tall timber there are views of rocky slopes above, dense forest below and Flagstaff in the distance. Bring binocs for views and wildlife up close. Fall also brings out huge bugling elk gathering harems for rut. You may spy bear, deer or wild turkey, but don't be mistaken for a cow elk. Could be trouble!

Kachina Trail traverses the mountain in a generally downhill direction. You must return the way you came, use two cars or enlist the support of a willing couch potato to drive shuttle.

DIRECTIONS: North out of Flag 7 miles on HWY 180 to milepost 223. Go right at Snow Bowl Road for 6.5 miles then turn right to the end of the parking area. If you use two cars or a shuttle, meet at Schultz Tank on Schultz Pass Road.

KENDRICK MOUNTAIN

KENDRICK LOOKOUT
ELEV. 10,400'

VIEW

CABIN

KENDRICK MTN. TRAIL

KENDRICK MOUNTAIN

4.6 MILES

ELEV. 7980'

0.5 MILES

190

START

171

3.1 MILES

TO GRAND CANYON 62 MILES

180

3.1 MILES

245

MILE POST 230

-LEGEND-

PAVED ROAD

DIRT ROAD

TRAIL

190 FOREST ROAD

P PARKING/ TRAILHEAD

N

NOT TO -SCALE-

TO FLAGSTAFF 14 MILES

FLAGSTAFF

KENDRICK MOUNTAIN TRAIL
GRADUAL CLIMB TO VAST VIEW

DISTANCE: 9.2 MILES
TIME: 4 TO 5 HOURS
EFFORT: SOME SWEAT
TYPE: UP THEN DOWN
FIND ROUTE: EASY
SEASON: APR to OCT

DESCRIPTION: This is a mighty fine gradual uphill ramble through some of the most prime aspen stands in Arizona to views of the San Francisco Peaks, The Grand Canyon to the north and Oak Creek Canyon to the south. Fall colors run amuck. The last magic days of September and first of October find Kendrick Mountain Trail paved red and gold while a few die- hards still hang sun lit and shimmering in the trees.

The trail is well marked, well used and the trail-head is easy to find. START with an easy grade up through thick forest for the first bit. As you start to switchback up the steeper slopes, the woods become much more pristine with big old fat Doug Fir, Engelmann Spruce and great sprawling stands of aspen. Just before the top you find an old forest service cabin from 1912. Poke around and write something funny in the register for me to read.

Look and listen for the bugle of elk in fall rut looking for new girlfriends. Carry water and food. Wear a hat for sun. Protective clothing is also a must for possible ice cold and very heavy sudden summer rain we call The Monsoon. Brrr!

DIRECTIONS: North out of Flag on HWY 180 toward the Grand Canyon. Go 14 miles to milepost 230 and turn LEFT onto FS 245. The roads are good. Follow the map to the trailhead.

LAVA RIVER CAVE

© 1999
RAY

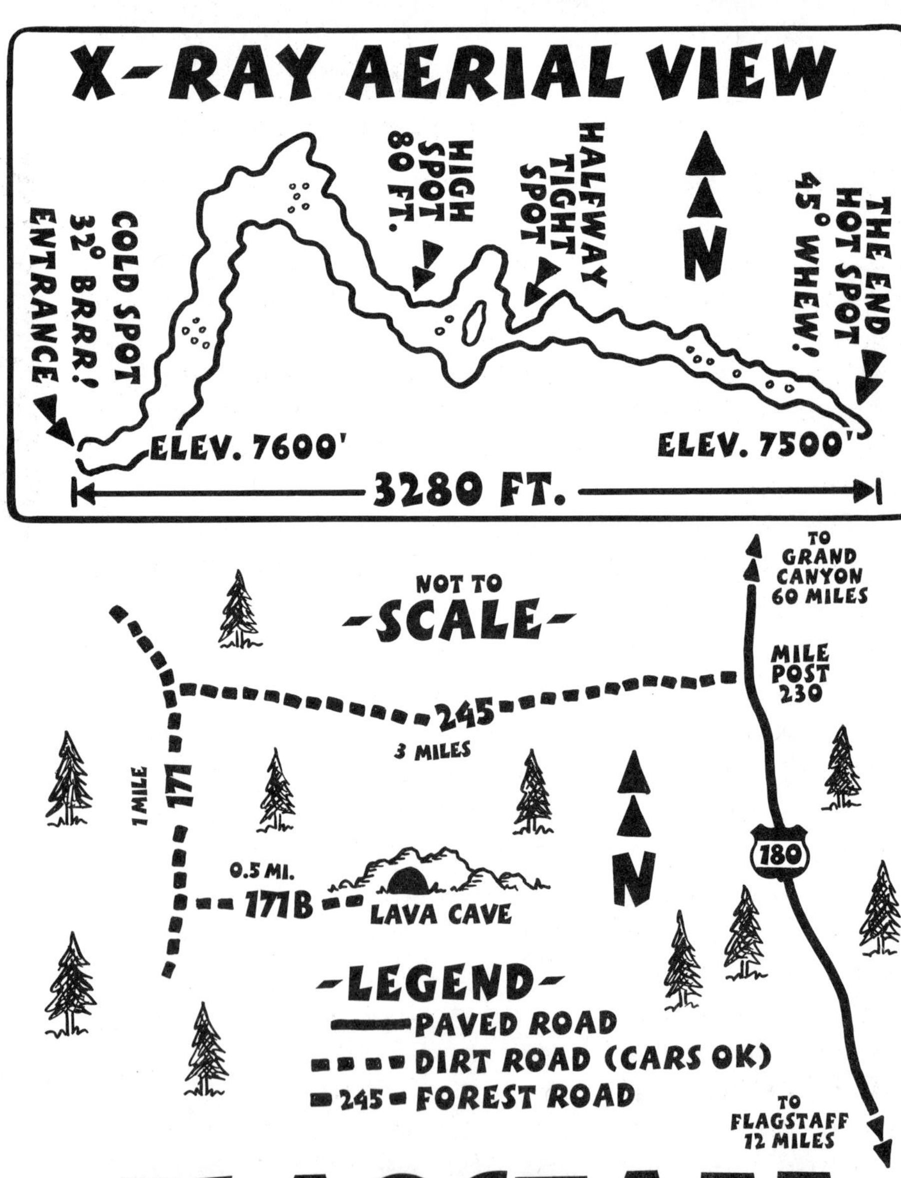

FLAGSTAFF

LAVA RIVER CAVE
DEEP & DARK CAVE ADVENTURE

DISTANCE: 1.4 MILES
TIME: 1 TO 1.5 HOURS
EFFORT: EASY/SCARY
TYPE: EXPLORE CAVE
FIND ROUTE: EASY/DARK
SEASON: APR to NOV

DESCRIPTION: This long lava tube cave was formed 700,000 years ago by molten rock that erupted from a volcanic vent in nearby Hart Prairie. The walls solidified first while the lava continued to flow and the tube emptied out. Ripples in the floor show where the last trickles flowed and stone icicles hang from the ceiling where a last blast of heat caused walls to drip.

If you freak easy, stay home because this hike quickly turns blacker than the inside of your cat at midnight. Carry two or three flashlights plus a pocket full of spare copper tops . Bring a coat, even in summer. Wear shoes, not sandals as the floor is paved with sharp slippery rocks.

Quite roomy on the inside with only one fairly tight squeeze at halfway, the ceiling reaches up 80 ft. in one spot. Be careful, it's cold and icy right when you enter. Drops 100 ft. over a distance of 3820 ft. to the end where it's always a balmy 45 degrees and very, very dark . Nice and quiet too.

DIRECTIONS: Go north out of Flag on Highway 180 toward Grand Canyon for 15 miles to milepost 230. Go left onto forest road 245 and follow the map to the cave. Dr. Ray says enjoy a sunny walk before and after.

FLAGSTAFF

LITTLE BEAR TRAIL

TO HYW 180 6 MILES

UPPER OLDHAM TRAIL

TO ELDEN LOOKOUT 1 MILE

ELDEN LOOKOUT ROAD

557

ELEV. 8800'

4.0 MI

SUNSET TRAIL

0.7 MI

CATWALK

VIEW

LITTLE BEAR TRAIL

VIEW

RADIO FIRE BURN 1978

0.9 MI

SCHULTZ PASS 2 MILES

HEART TRAIL 2.5 MI

VIEW

-SCALE-

1/2 MI

0.3

START

P

ELEV. 7400'

SANDY SEEP

SEEP TRAIL

LITTLE ELDEN TRAIL

2.9 MI

ELDEN SPRING ROAD

2.5 MI

556

-LEGEND-

PAVED ROAD

GOOD DIRT ROAD

TRAIL

P PARKING/ TRAILHEAD

SANDY

TO FLAGSTAFF 1 MILE

P

ELEV. 7000'

ELEV. 7000'

89

TO PAGE

MILE POST 421.1

MILE POST 423.3

FLAGSTAFF

LITTLE BEAR TRAIL
SECLUDED FOREST TRAIL ON MT. ELDEN

DISTANCE: 10.4 MILES
TIME: 3 TO 4 HOURS
EFFORT: DIFFICULT
TYPE: OUT & BACK
FIND ROUTE: EASY
SEASON: MAY to NOV

CONTOUR PROFILE

FLAGSTAFF

DESCRIPTION: Green and shady Little Bear rolls relentlessly but gradually uphill for every bit of its 5.2 mile length from the trailhead. However, what goes up . . . well, you know the rest. Its smooth surface and gradual gradient make it a real favorite among the local equestrians, hikers and mountain bikers. Conifers and aspen line the way. Great views.

Constructed within the last couple of years, you will marvel at how much hand work went into this trailbuilder's masterwork. It's an engineering feat. Little Bear climbs from the trailhead on Elden Spring Road, crosses Little Elden Trail and then switchbacks up to where it intersects Sunset Trail. From there you can connect the dots and put together all manner of loops on Mt. Elden's superb trail system.

Little Bear is on the remote, shady north side of Elden. That means fewer people and snow that lasts well into spring, but always nice and cool during the warmest days of summer. Be prepared for afternoon rain during July and August monsoon season. Watch out for bikes and horses on weekends.

DIRECTIONS: Go north out of Flagstaff on HWY 89 headed toward Page. About 3 miles out of town turn LEFT onto FS 556, Elden Springs Road, at milepost 423.3. Go another 2.5 miles to the well marked trailhead parking area on the right.

MOUNT ELDEN LOOKOUT

© 1999 RAY

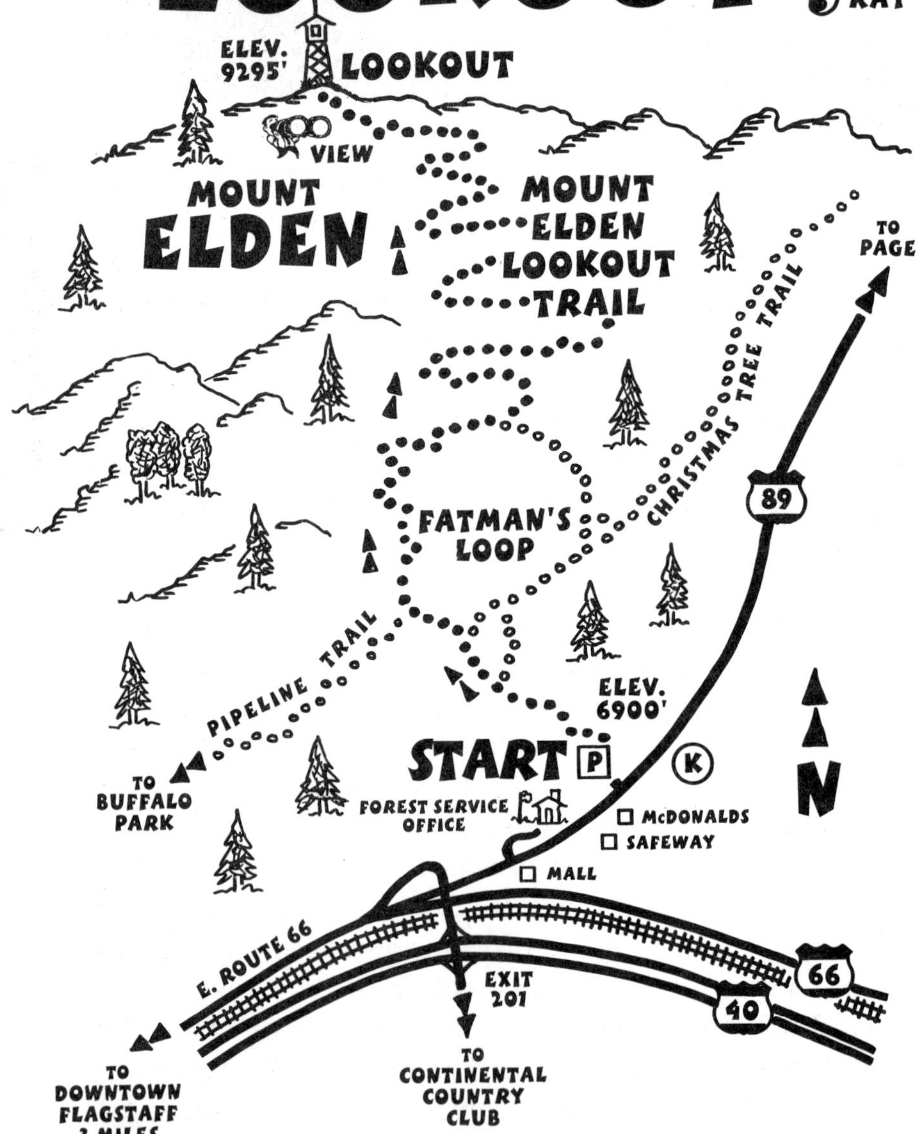

FLAGSTAFF

LOOKOUT TRAIL

STUDLY CLIMB TO KILLER ELDEN VIEW

DISTANCE: 6 MILES
TIME: 4 to 5 HOURS
EFFORT: IT'S A TUFFY
TYPE: OUT & BACK
FIND ROUTE: EASY
SEASON: APR to NOV

DESCRIPTION: "Corduroy cast in stone" is how the southeastern face of Mt. Elden has been described. The Elden Lookout Trail trail has been called a "staircase of petrified lava". Cool! That should get you psyched, but there's more. Airplane views of Flagstaff, eastern Arizona and the Elden Burn make this hike epic.

A fire lookout ranger ran for his life in 1977 when a fire toasted the tower along with the entire top and eastern slope of Elden. Hollow, bleached bones of an ancient forest still stand, but aspen now spring up everywhere. A view of Elden's volcanic geology and eons of erosion is clearly visible.

The trail begins as a gradual stroll through fragrant pinon and juniper up Fat Man's Loop for the first mile. At the top of Fat Man's, the lookout trail takes off steep for the next 2 miles to the top. Bring food, water and protective clothing. Weather can be severe up here. Hot sun, strong wind and heavy rain are likely any summer day. Boiling black clouds and crackling bolts of lightning are best viewed from a healthy distance.

DIRECTIONS: From downtown Flag go 3 miles east on Route 66 through East Flag. Continue toward Page on Highway 89. Mt. Elden Trailhead is on your left just past Safeway and Micky D's.

FLAGSTAFF

OBSERVATORY MESA

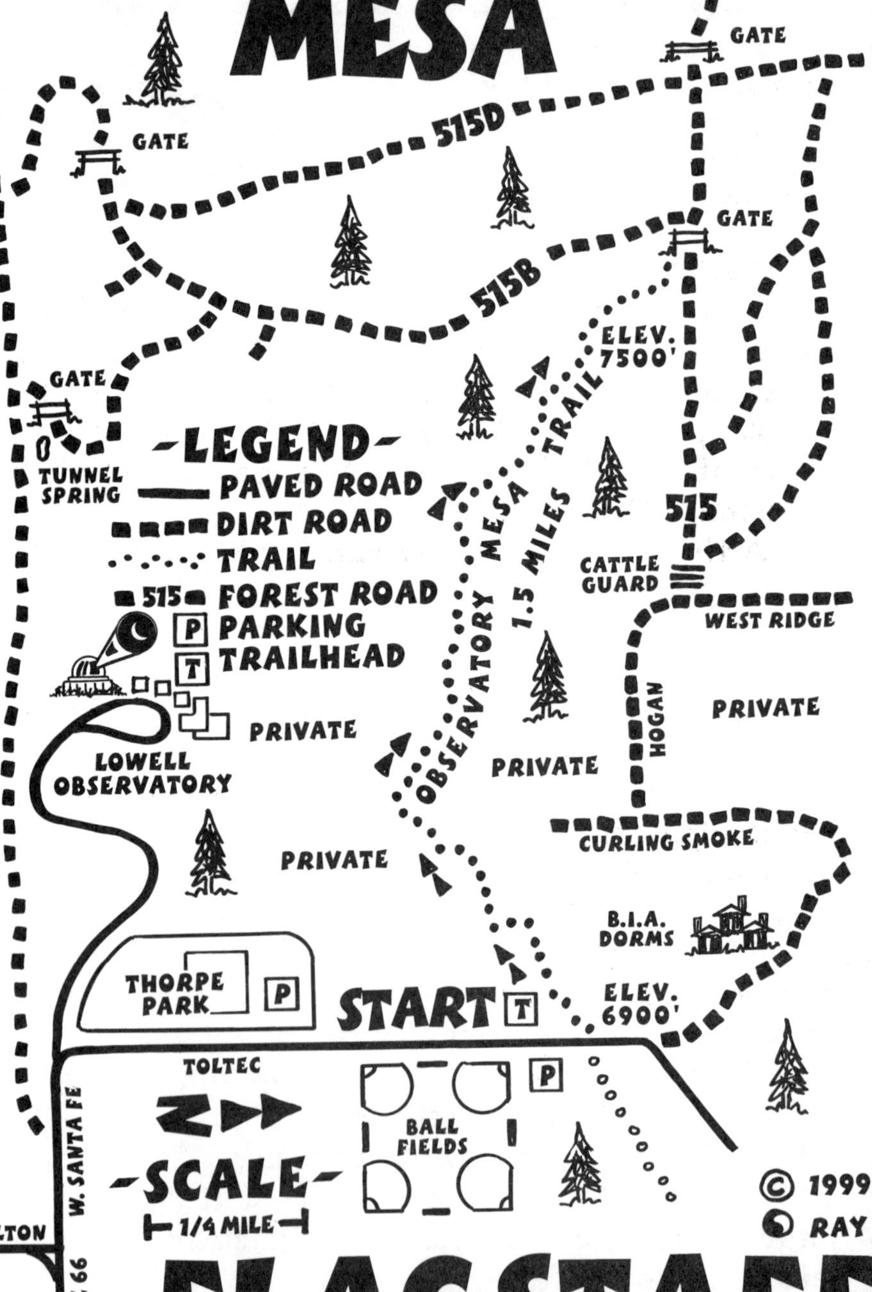

FLAGSTAFF

OBSERVATORY MESA
SCENIC TRAILS VERY CLOSE TO TOWN

DISTANCE: 3 MILES
TIME: 1 to 3 HOURS
EFFORT: ONE STEEP HILL
TYPE: OUT & BACK
FIND ROUTE: EASY
SEASON: MAR to NOV

CONTOUR PROFILE

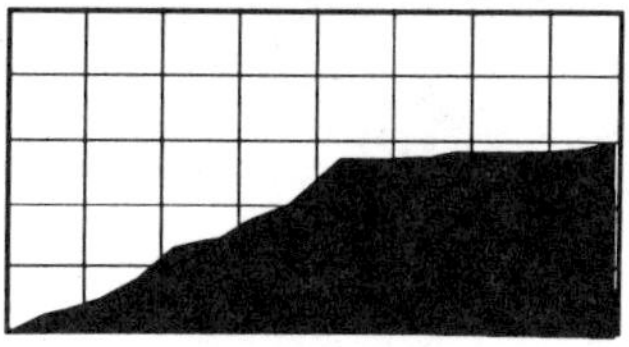

7900
ELEV. (FT.)
6900
0 **1-WAY MILES** 1.5

DESCRIPTION: Atop Lowell Observatory Mesa is Flag's fave place to hike, bike, run, ski, snowshoe or walk the dog *AND* it's only a stone's throw from downtown. These 15 square miles of USFS land are just west of town up behind Lowell Observatory.

Local hunters would be alarmed to learn how close their sought after elk herds safely come to their backyard gardens. Spring and fall migrations bring these magnificent beasts over the mesa by the thousands on their way to and from Arizona's high country. Any morning or evening stroll is guaranteed a sighting of at least one 1000 lb. hatrack!

Access has been made simple by an addition to Flagstaff's Urban Trail System. A smooth, wide and hard packed cinder track from a parking lot near the ball fields on Toltec Ave. (see map) leads up 600 ft. onto the mesa. It's a good grunt to get up, but once there everything is flat or downhill. Use the map to create your own loop. You can't get too lost. Look through the tree tops for a view of The Peaks. That's North.

DIRECTIONS: You can see from the map that the trail is less than a mile from downtown. Park in the lot by the north end of the ball fields. The trail is across the street and heads up the hill. Watch for mountain bikers speeding down.

OLDHAM TRAIL

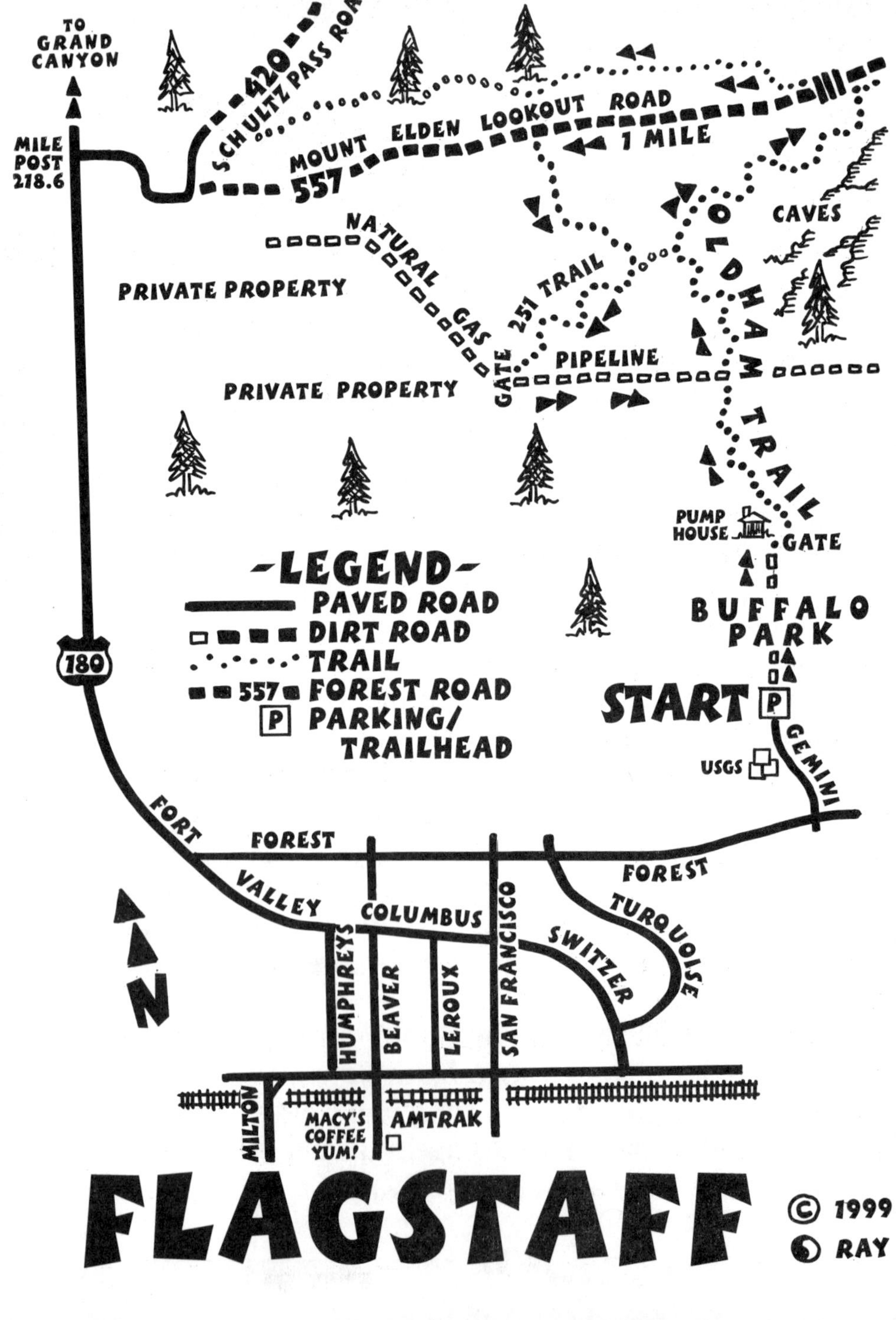

TO GRAND CANYON

MILE POST 218.6

420 SCHULTZ PASS ROAD

MOUNT ELDEN LOOKOUT ROAD

557

1 MILE

CAVES

NATURAL GAS PIPELINE

PRIVATE PROPERTY

251 TRAIL

GATE

OLDHAM TRAIL

PRIVATE PROPERTY

PUMP HOUSE

GATE

BUFFALO PARK

-LEGEND-

PAVED ROAD
DIRT ROAD
TRAIL
557 FOREST ROAD
P PARKING/ TRAILHEAD

180

START P

USGS

GEMINI

FORT VALLEY

FOREST

FOREST

N

COLUMBUS

TURQUOISE

SWITZER

HUMPHREYS

BEAVER

LEROUX

SAN FRANCISCO

MILTON

MACY'S COFFEE YUM!

AMTRAK

FLAGSTAFF

OLDHAM TRAIL LOOP
NICE ROLLING STROLL NEAR TOWN

DISTANCE: 5 MILES
TIME: 2 to 2.5 HOURS
EFFORT: MODERATE
TYPE: LOOP
FIND ROUTE: EASY
SEASON: MAR to NOV

FLAGSTAFF

DESCRIPTION: Scenic boulder fields, cliffs, caves and forest. Traces an idyllic, winding, singletrack under a canopy of tall pines. Close to town. Oldham Trail leads from Flag's favorite urban park into the Mount Elden trail system directly north of town. Oldham is well signed, but to turn this hike into a nice 5-mile loop there is a trick or two. Follow instructions closely.

BEGIN in Buffalo Park, Flagstaff's urban forest park, at the buffalo statue. Cross the park going north, STRAIGHT for Mt. Elden. CONTINUE out the back gate just behind a gas pumphouse. The trail heads down a rocky, rooted single track and continue until you encounter a gas pipeline road at the 1 mile point. CONTINUE across this clearing and follow the sign up and over a steep ridge and down the other side. Go RIGHT at the bottom and CONTINUE up to Mt. Elden Lookout Road at the 2 mile point. All signed so far.

Go LEFT down Elden Road a mile to obvious but unmarked trail on left at the 3 mile mark. Go LEFT and continue on this broad trail, ignoring false side trails, until you again hit pipeline road at a sign that says "251". Go LEFT and soon hit the trail you came down from Buffalo Park at the 4 mile point. Go RIGHT back up to Buffalo Park and BACK TO GO.

DIRECTIONS: Easy to find trailhead. From downtown Flagstaff go north on N. San Francisco Street toward The Peaks. Turn right on Forest Ave. Go left at the top of the hill onto Gemini and park at the Buffalo.

RED MOUNTAIN

ELEV. 7965'

RED MTN.

CUTAWAY

ELEV. 7300'

THE GATEWAY

TO GRAND CANYON 45 MILES

PREVENT EROSION

STAY ON TRAILS

ELEV. 7000'

START P

9023V 0.3 MILES

180

MILE POST 247

TO FLAGSTAFF 30 MILES

LEGEND

PAVED ROAD

DIRT ROAD (CARS OK)

TRAIL

9023V FOREST ROAD

P PARKING/TRAILHEAD

N

SCALE

1/4 MILE

FLAGSTAFF

RED MOUNTAIN
EASY HIKE TO *INSIDE* A MOUNTAIN

DISTANCE: 2.6 MILES
TIME: 1 TO 2 HOURS
EFFORT: EASY
TYPE: OUT & BACK
FIND ROUTE: EASY
SEASON: MAR to NOV

CONTOUR PROFILE

7500
ELEV. (FT.)
7000

0 **1-WAY MILES** 1.3

FLAGSTAFF

DESCRIPTION: Red Mountain is like all the other small mountains or volcanic cinder hills that dot this area north of The San Francisco Peaks *except* its eastern face has collapsed and fallen away revealing a cutaway core.

Bring binoculars. If I were a bird, I'd live here! The exposed cliffs of *The Cutaway* are covered with *juecos* or big swiss cheese holes caused by gas bubbles as the mountain was formed making for hundreds of bird condos. Hoodoos and goblins with eye holes look for all the world like a chorus of Mr. Potato Heads keeping their eyes on you. Redrock flutes, slots and butt cracks are everywhere on the eroded cliff face. Summer mornings are best for viewing and photos of this mondo bizarro scene.

The easy, well marked trail heads up an old road then into a wash at 0.8 miles and continues. At 1.2 miles you meet a 7 ft. high rock dam blocking *The Gateway*. Up and over or go up the nearby steep cinder path. Continue just a few more feet and you're there. Explore, but use caution. The surfaces of this steep scenery are NOT suitable for climbing and may flake off in your hand. Stay on trails or slickrock. Footprints begin new avenues for erosion leaving ugly scars.

DIRECTIONS: North out of Flag on Highway 180 for 30 miles to milepost 247. Follow map to the parking area.

SUNSET TRAIL

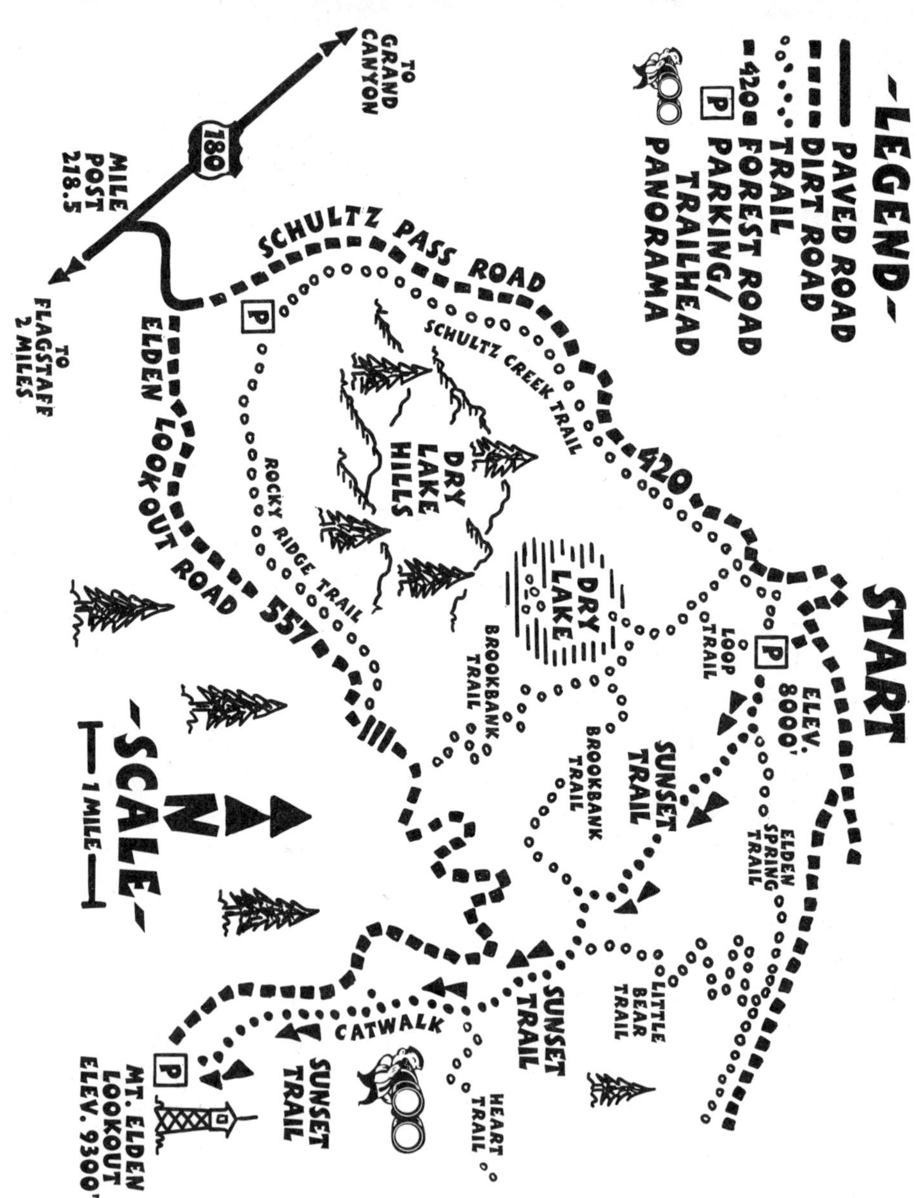

FLAGSTAFF

SUNSET TRAIL
KILLER VIEW FROM NARROW CATWALK

DISTANCE: 8 MILES
TIME: 4 TO 5 HOURS
EFFORT: DIFFICULT
TYPE: OUT & BACK
FIND ROUTE: EASY
SEASON: APR to NOV

FLAGSTAFF

DESCRIPTION: A vast panorama stretches from Sunset Crater and the volcanic fields just east of Flagstaff clear to Indian Country and the Painted Desert 100 miles out. North set The San Francisco Peaks. Below is what remains of the 1977 wildfire that cooked the top off Mt. Elden. After 20 years many of the hollow, sun bleached skeletons of ancient giants still stand as tens of thousands of aspen spring up and life goes on. The volcanic cliffs, spires, hoodoos and weird formations of Mt. Elden and Little Elden Mountain now stand exposed.

These days, all your turns are well signed, so no need to worry about getting lost. BEGIN at Schultz Tank, a rare-in-these-parts alpine lake, and go up through a north facing and thus lush forest. At the 1.5 mile point encounter a trail junction and go LEFT downhill, then climb up steep thru a fern forest until you come out on a narrow cat walk overlooking the burn and those vast views at the 3 mile mark. Now just eek your way along the ridge and see trail's end ahead at the 4 mile point at the Elden Lookout tower. Return the way you came and hike Sunset as a very long out & back OR use two cars for a great mere moderate hike.

DIRECTIONS: From downtown Flagstaff go north 3 miles on Highway 180 to milepost 218.6. Turn right and go up Schultz Pass Road 5.5 miles to the top and turn into the signed trailhead parking area on the right.

VIET SPRINGS LOOP

© 2001
RAY

TO SNOWBOWL SKI AREA 2 MILES

ELEV. 8600'

START

GATE

P

MILE 4.5

SNOW BOWL ROAD

TO HWY 180 AT MILEPOST 223

WIDE TRAIL

SMALL FOOT TRAIL

POWERLINE

N

ESCARPMENT

PICTO GRAPHS

CANADIAN SPRING

VIET SPRING

SHED

CABIN

CABIN SITE

MONUMENT

-LEGEND-

PAVED ROAD

TRAIL

P PARKING/ TRAILHEAD

FLAGSTAFF

VEIT SPRINGS LOOP

PEAKS STROLL TO SPRINGS & PICTOGRAPHS

DISTANCE: 2 MILE LOOP
TIME: JUST 1 HOUR OR SO
EFFORT: EASY STROLL
TYPE: OUT & BACK OR LOOP
FIND ROUTE: EASY
SEASON: APR to NOV

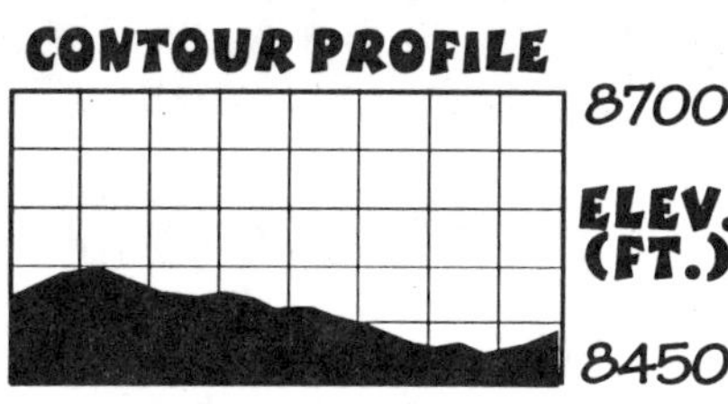

DESCRIPTION: In fall, this short stroll through aspen and old growth pine to Veit Springs looks to be a gilded illustration from an old time children's book. In spring, sunlight glows bright, bright green through young leaves. In summer the aspen shimmer and quake in the breeze. Veit springs attract a wide variety of wildlife. If you are early and quiet you will for certain see elk. Birdsong is always in the air. Tall ferns as well as purple, red, blue, white and yellow wildflowers are everywhere. The hike is short and fairly level, so young kids are able to tag along on foot or in a kiddie pack without much effort.

If you follow the map, you make a nice little loop. First stop is Ludwig Veit's 1890s cabin. His name is etched in a nearby boulder just to the right of the cabin. Up behind the cabin is another old stone shed. Veit Spring flows out of the escarpment just up behind that. Walk to the left along the escarpment for another 150 feet and you come to Canadian Spring. Look for a few faint pictographs left by the ancients in the rock above the spring.

DIRECTIONS: Leave Flagstaff going toward The Grand Canyon on HWY 180 for about 7 miles to milepost 223. Turn RIGHT and head up Snow Bowl Road for 4.5 miles. Park in the lot in front of the trailhead gate.

WALNUT CANYON
NATIONAL MONUMENT

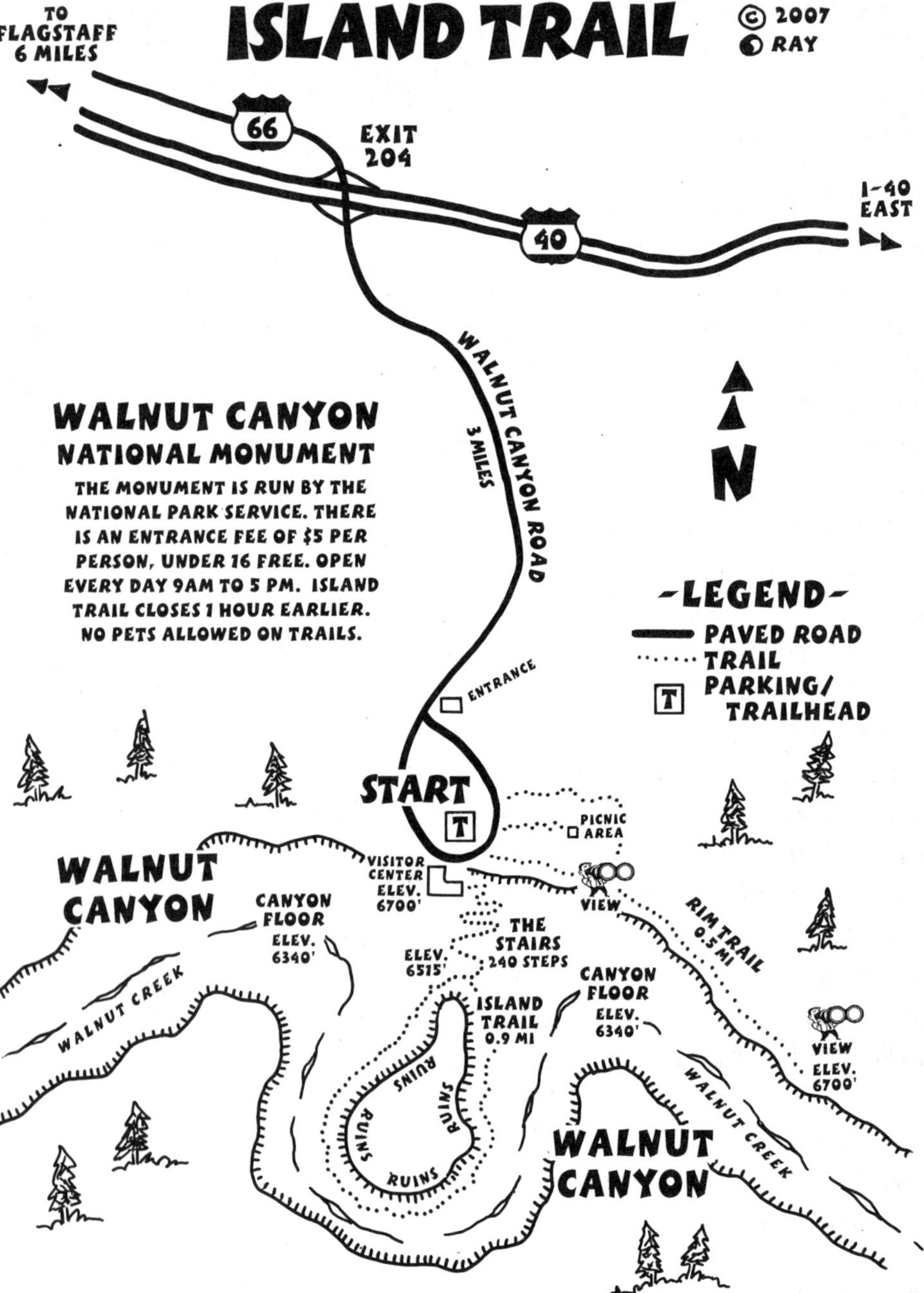

WALNUT CANYON

ISLAND TRAIL VISITS 25 CLIFF DWELLER RUINS

ISLAND TRAIL

DISTANCE: 0.9 MILES
TIME: 1 HOUR
EFFORT: SHORT & STEEP
240 STEPS GAIN 185' ELEVATION
TYPE: LOOP
FIND ROUTE: VERY EASY
SEASON: OPEN ALL YEAR
CLOSED WHEN TRAIL IS ICY

CONTOUR PROFILE

DESCRIPTION: The Sinagua cliff dwellers left their shelters built into the limestone walls of walnut Canyon 800 years ago. The name "Sinagua" is derived from the Spanish words meaning "without water", so called because The Sinagua were able to create a hunting and farming existence in this relatively dry landscape.

Their homes were built into the south and east side of the canyon walls to take advantage of sunlight and warmth. A few sites on the north and west site were probably used to escape summer heat. They took advantage of caves that had been eroded out of the limestone cliffs by water and wind. To improve the natural caves, they shaped rocks to form walls and cemented them together with clay and re-enforced doorways with timber. The walls were plastered with clay both inside and out. Island Trail leads you down 240 steps to a loop passing by 25 such dwellings. Stay on the trail at all times. Touch nothing. Nearby Rim Trail is much easier with great views of the canyon walls.

DIRECTIONS: Easy to find. From anywhere in Flagstaff get on I-40 heading East . Go 6 miles to Exit #240 and follow the signs to Walnut Canyon National Monument.

WEATHERFORD TRAIL

N
SCALE
1 MI.

1.0 MI.
HUMPHREYS PEAK 12,633'
HUMPHREYS PEAK TRAIL
11,800'
INNER BASIN
TO ARIZONA SNOWBOWL 3 MILES
FREMONT SADDLE 10,800'
DOYLE PEAK 11,460'
AGASSIZ PEAK 12,356'
DOYLE SADDLE 11,354'
FREMONT PEAK 11,969'
8.1 MI.
10,400'
TO ARIZONA SNOWBOWL 5 MILES
KACHINA TRAIL
SCHULTZ PEAK 10,083'
ASPEN SPRING 8852'
TO SNOWBOWL ROAD AT MILEPOST 2.5 3.5 MILES
0.7 MI.
FREIDLEIN PRAIRIE ROAD
FS 522
1.6 MI.
P

-LEGEND-

- DIRT ROAD (ALL CARS OK)
- JEEP ROAD
- WEATHERFORD TRAIL
- OTHER SYSTEM TRAIL
- P TRAILHEAD/ PARKING

MAP ADAPTED FROM HUMPHREYS PEAK USGS 7.5' QUAD

SCHULTZ PASS ROAD
FS 420
TO HWY 180 MILEPOST 218.5
P
SCHULTZ TANK 8,024'
START

FLAGSTAFF

WEATHERFORD TRAIL
EASY OR EPIC ADVENTURE ON THE PEAKS

DISTANCE: 3 to 20 MILES
TIME: 2 to 9 HOURS
EFFORT: EASY to WHEW!
TYPE: OUT & BACK
ROUTE FINDING: EASY
SEASON: APR to OCT

CONTOUR PROFILE

DESCRIPTION: Don't freak. You don't have to hike all the way to the top of The Peaks. The Weatherford Trail is an out-and-back, or up-and-down as the case may be. You can do a short little 1.6mile stroll just up to Aspen Spring, check out the fall colors and then run back down to the safety of your car.

However, I warn you. Though no law says you must go further, you will see the trail disappearing into the aspen and up the side of The San Francisco Peaks. It's pretty darn near irresistible not to continue at least a little further. The higher you go, the higher you get.

If you make it as far as Fremont Saddle at 10,800' , you'll have a great hike. Continue to Doyle Saddle at 11,354' and you'll have done a mighty-dog day's work. From there it's only a short bit to where the Humphrey's Peak Trail comes in at 11,800'. "Might as well go to the top" I can hear you say, but don't be fooled, that last mile to 12,633' is one tough mutha grunt when you're pooped and out of supplies. It's a loooong way back to the car.

As the views indicate, you are way high up on this hike. You are in outer space. No man or woman's land. Be prepared. Do not hike here when dark clouds boil up the summer monsoon cauldron. Some fool is killed by lightning right here nearly every year. Fall is best. Begin early in the day. Bring lotsa water, good boots, grub and gear.

DIRECTIONS: Go north out of Flag on HWY 180 to Schultz Pass Road at milepost 218.5. Go up Schultz Pass Road 5 miles to the parking lot at Schultz Tank. The trail is well signed and takes off toward The Peaks just across the road.

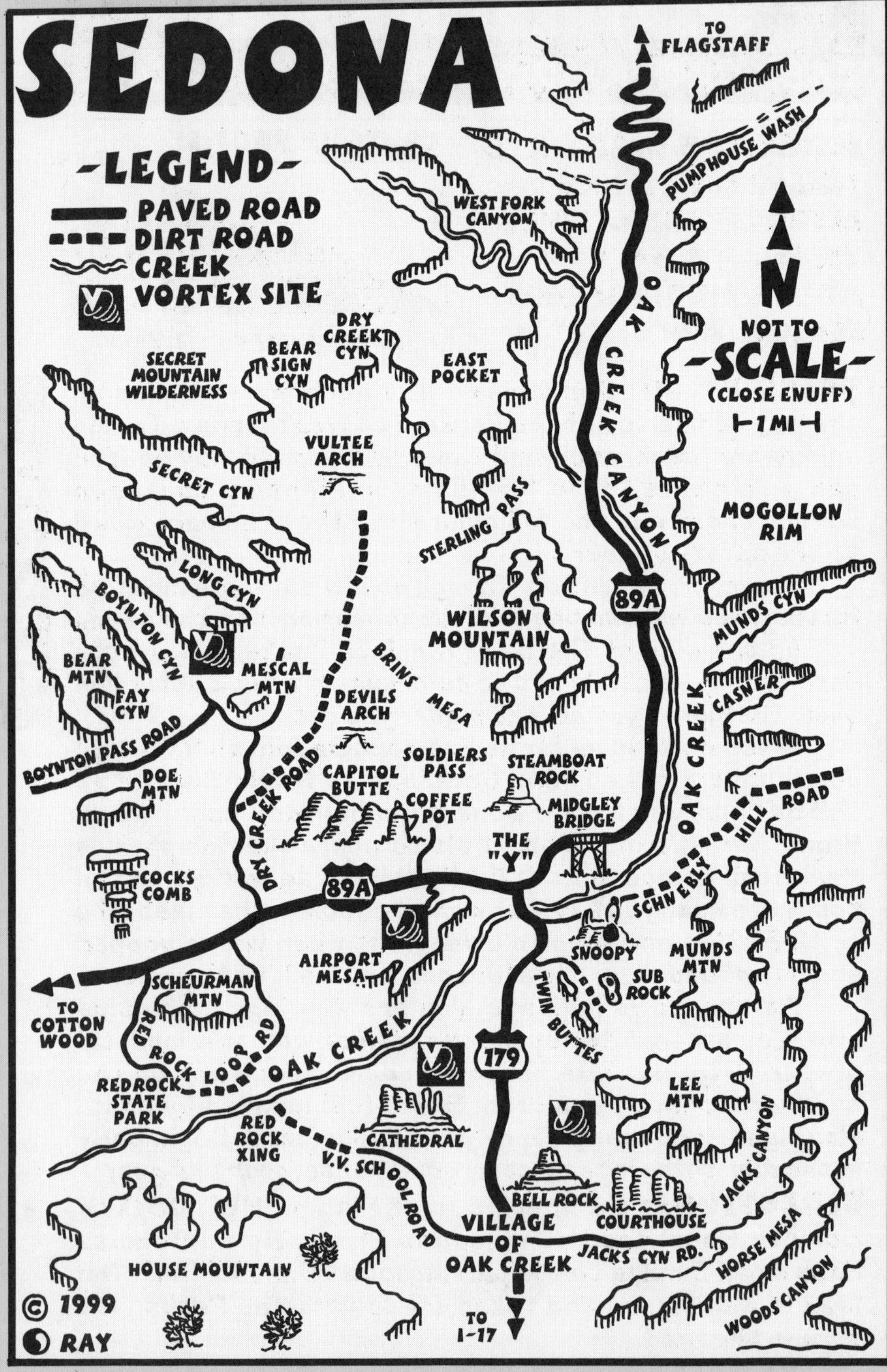
SEDONA
-LEGEND-
PAVED ROAD
DIRT ROAD
CREEK
VORTEX SITE
TO FLAGSTAFF
PUMPHOUSE WASH
WEST FORK CANYON
OAK CREEK CANYON
N
NOT TO
-SCALE-
(CLOSE ENUFF)
1 MI
DRY CREEK CYN
BEAR SIGN CYN
SECRET MOUNTAIN WILDERNESS
EAST POCKET
VULTEE ARCH
SECRET CYN
STERLING PASS
MOGOLLON RIM
LONG CYN
BOYNTON CYN
89A
WILSON MOUNTAIN
MUNDS CYN
BEAR MTN
FAY CYN
MESCAL MTN
BRINS MESA
DEVILS ARCH
CASNER
OAK CREEK
BOYNTON PASS ROAD
DOE MTN
DRY CREEK ROAD
CAPITOL BUTTE
SOLDIERS PASS
STEAMBOAT ROCK
COFFEE POT
MIDGLEY BRIDGE
SCHNEBLY HILL ROAD
THE "Y"
COCKS COMB
89A
SNOOPY
MUNDS MTN
AIRPORT MESA
SUB ROCK
TWIN BUTTES
TO COTTON WOOD
SCHEURMAN MTN
RED ROCK LOOP RD
OAK CREEK
179
REDROCK STATE PARK
LEE MTN
RED ROCK XING
CATHEDRAL
JACKS CANYON
V.V. SCHOOL ROAD
BELL ROCK
COURTHOUSE
VILLAGE OF OAK CREEK
JACKS CYN RD.
HORSE MESA
HOUSE MOUNTAIN
WOODS CANYON
© 1999
RAY
TO I-17

THE WEATHER*

	JAN	FEB	MAR	APR	MAY	JUN	JUL	AUG	SEP	OCT	NOV	DEC	
AVERAGE MAXIMUM DAILY TEMPERATURES (°F)													AVG
Flagstaff	41.8	44.8	48.6	57.5	66.6	77.7	81.6	78.9	73.9	63.8	51.2	44.0	60.9
Sedona	54.8	59L6	64.0	72.7	81.2	92.2	96.1	93.3	88.8	78.1	65.3	56.3	75.2
AVERAGE MINIMUM DAILY TEMPERATURES (°F)													AVG
Flagstaff	15.0	17.2	20.8	26.4	33.0	41.0	50.5	48.7	41.0	30.7	21.8	16.2	30.2
Sedona	29.1	31.6	34.5	40.7	47.5	56.3	63.9	62.4	57.1	47.4	36.3	39.7	44.7
HIGHEST RECORDED TEMPERATURE (°F) / YEAR OF OCCURRENCE													
Flagstaff	66/'71	70/'77	73/'66	68/'62	87/'51	96/'70	97/'73	97/'77	90/'50	85/'80	74/'73	68/'50	
Sedona	77/'71	88/'63	85/'66	93/'65	100/'51	110/'81	110/'81	108/'72	104/'48	100/'80	88/'65	77/'50	
LOWEST RECORDED TEMPERATURE (°F) / YEAR OF OCCURRENCE													
Flagstaff	-22/'71	-16/'55	-16/'66	-2/'75	14/'75	22/'51	32/'55	24/'68	23/'55	-2/'71	-13/'58	-23/'78	
Sedona	0/'62	10/'49	9/'71	18/'72	24/'75	36/'68	43/'68	45/'68	28/'68	26/'61	11/'70	0/'68	
AVERAGE MONTHLY PRECIPITATION (INCHES)													TOTAL
Flagstaff	2.2	1.9	2.3	1.3	.7	.6	2.5	2.6	1.5	1.5	1.8	2.2	21.1
Sedona	2.1	1.8	1.9	1.1	.6	.5	1.9	2.1	1.5	1.5	1.4	1.5	17.7
AVERAGE MONTHLY SNOWFALL (INCHES)													TOTAL
Flagstaff	19.9	15.7	22.2	10.1	2.2	0	0	0	.1	2.5	9.2	15.3	97.2
Sedona	2.4	.6	.8	0	0	0	0	0	0	0	0	1.9	5.9

*GLEANED FROM *ARIZONA CLIMATE: 100 YEARS*, UNIVERSITY OF ARIZONA PRESS

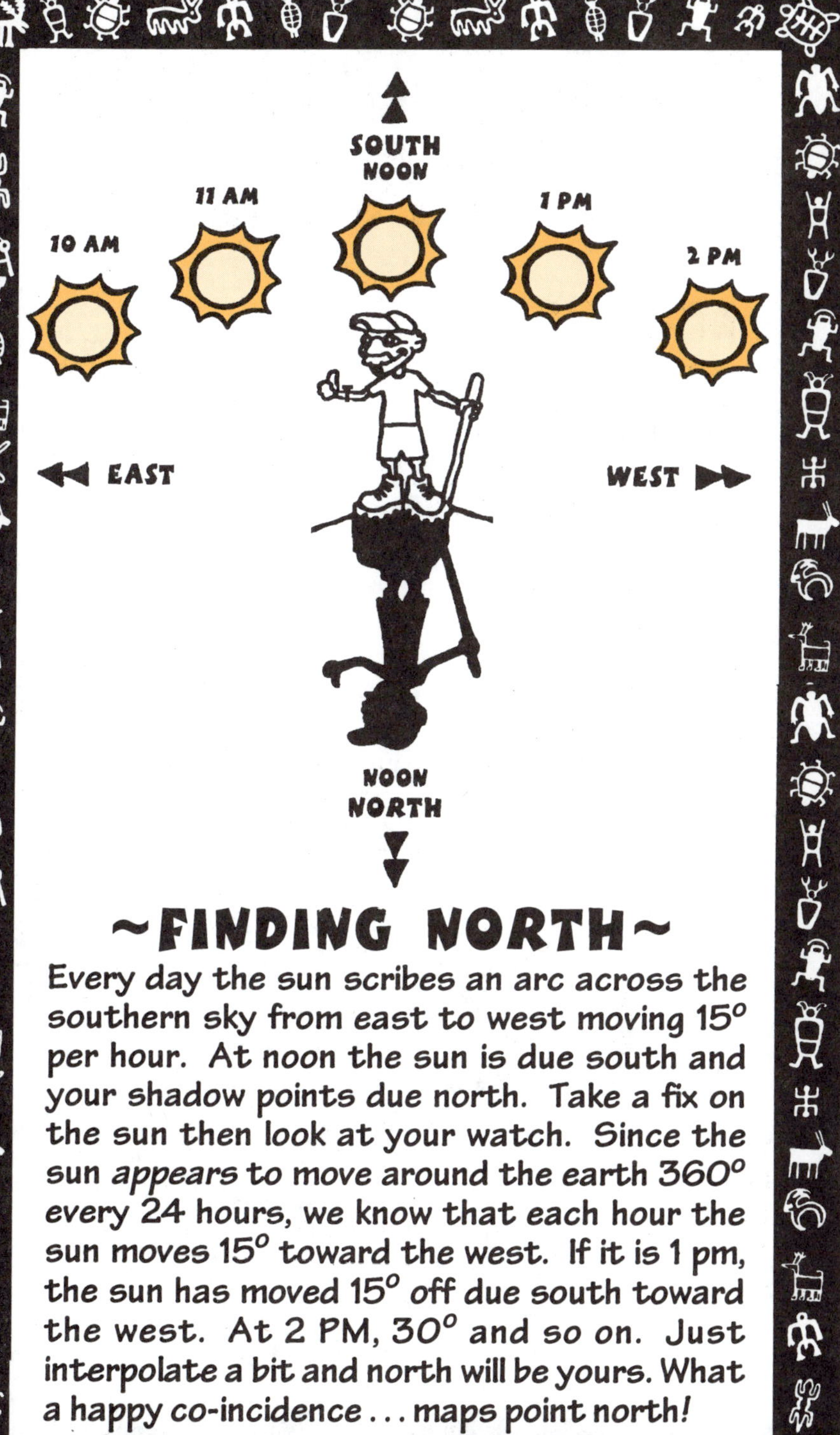

~FINDING NORTH~

Every day the sun scribes an arc across the southern sky from east to west moving 15° per hour. At noon the sun is due south and your shadow points due north. Take a fix on the sun then look at your watch. Since the sun *appears* to move around the earth 360° every 24 hours, we know that each hour the sun moves 15° toward the west. If it is 1 pm, the sun has moved 15° off due south toward the west. At 2 PM, 30° and so on. Just interpolate a bit and north will be yours. What a happy co-incidence . . . maps point north!

A.B. YOUNG TRAIL

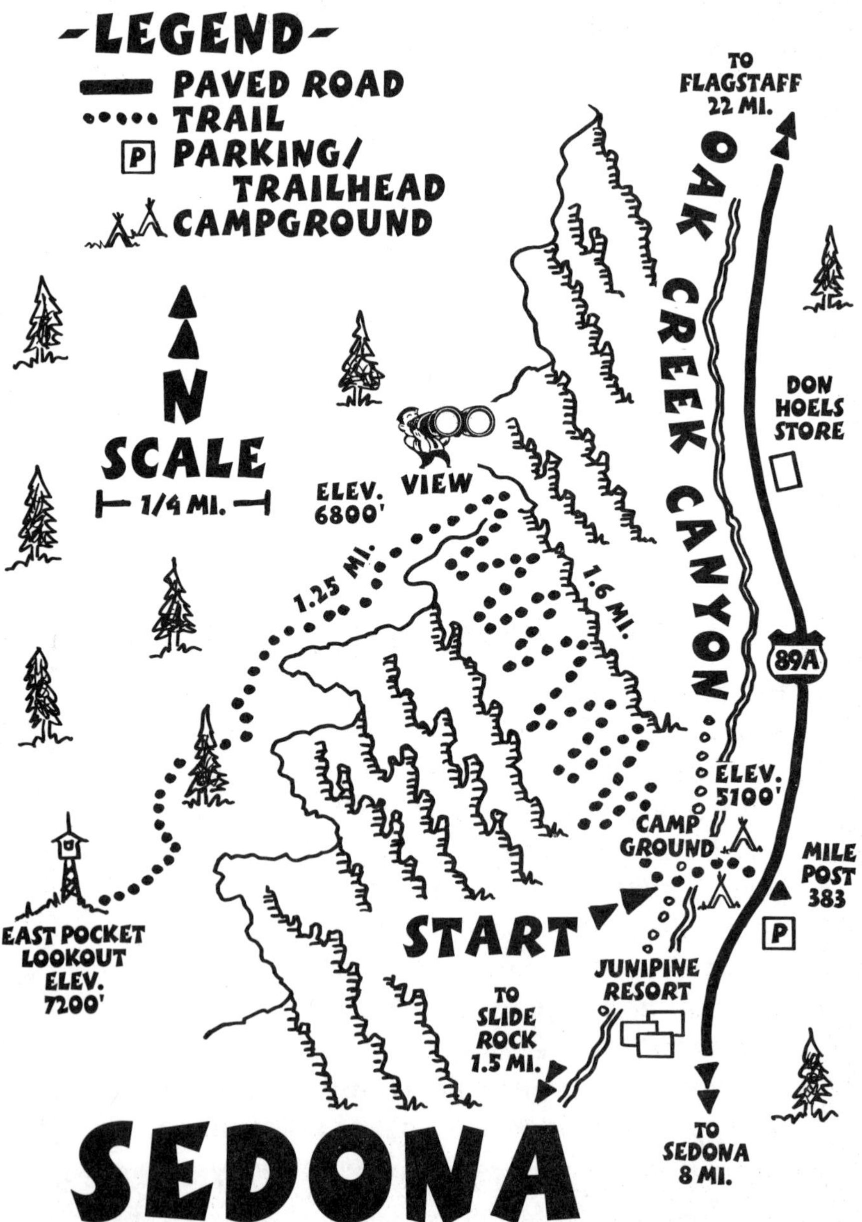

A.B.YOUNG TRAIL
QUICK UP & DOWN FROM OAK CREEK

DISTANCE: 3.2 MILES
TIME: 2 to 3.5 HOURS
EFFORT: SEMI-HARD
TYPE: OUT & BACK
ROUTE FINDING: EASY
SEASON: APR to NOV

DESCRIPTION: You be young too if you be fit enough to motor up these 33 tight switchbacks to the west rim of Oak Creek Canyon. Scope out fabulous views up, down and across Oak Creek. Catch your breath. If energy remains, go 1.25 miles further and more gradually ascend an additional 400 ft. to East Pocket fire lookout tower. A.B. Young zig-zags up an exposed south face so it can be relentlessly sunny and warm in summer. Wear a hat. Carry water and snack.

Best view and lunch spot is on the rocks right at the top of the switchbacks. The added stroll out to the lookout tower on a narrow forest single track is pleasant, but the view from the tower is obscured by nearby trees. The deck at Junipine Resort is great for kicking back and enjoying a bit of apres hike snackage.

DIRECTIONS: The trailhead is 8 miles north of Sedona or 21 miles south of Flagstaff on Highway 89A at milepost 383 near Bootlegger Campground. Park in a wide spot on 89A. Cross the campground and head directly down to and across Oak Creek via boulder hop. Don't make a splash! The rusty steel trailhead sign is just slightly downstream from Bootlegger. A.B. Young immediately takes off up and steep from the creek.

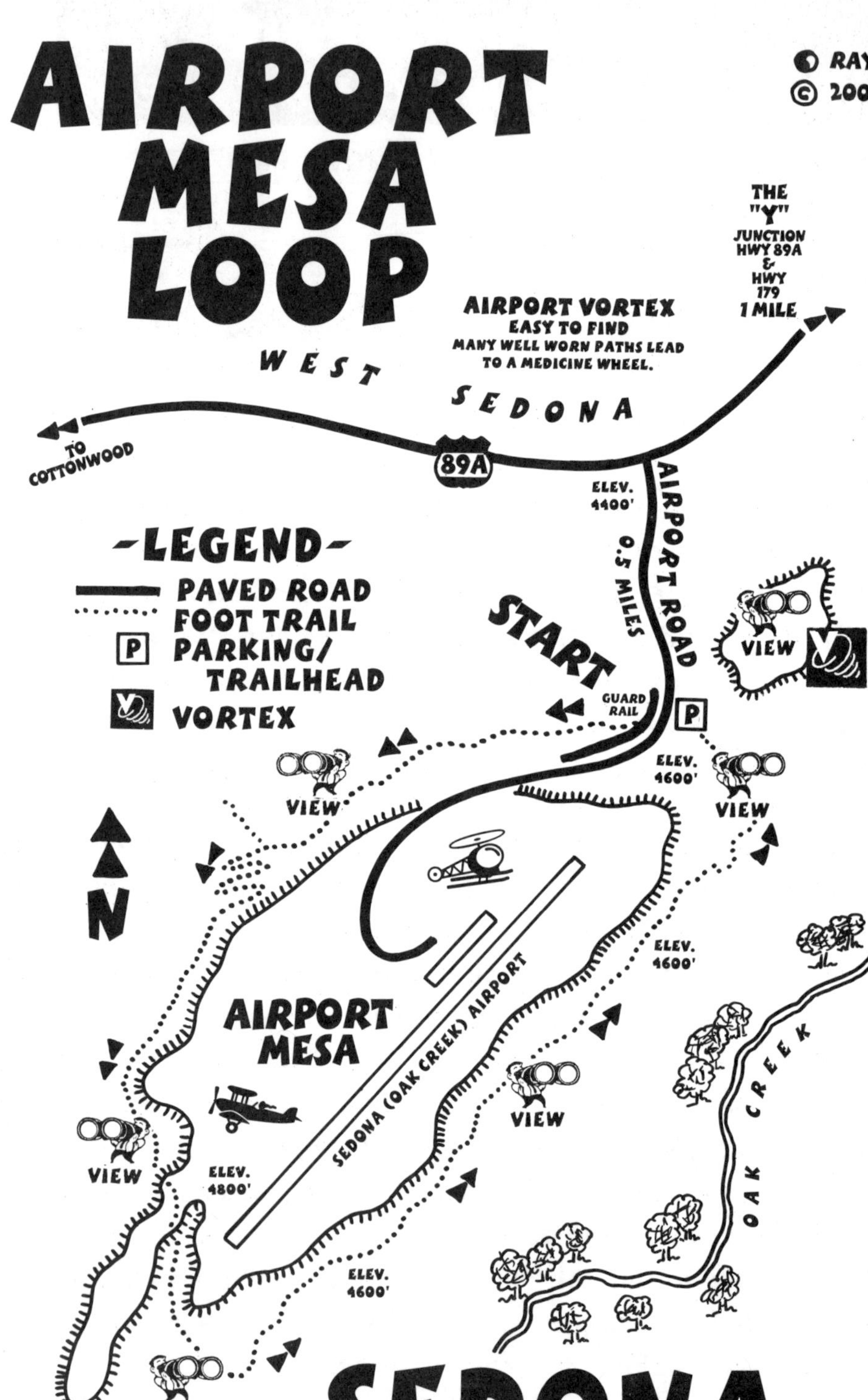

AIRPORT MESA LOOP
© RAY
© 2000
THE "Y" JUNCTION HWY 89A & HWY 179 1 MILE
AIRPORT VORTEX
EASY TO FIND
MANY WELL WORN PATHS LEAD
TO A MEDICINE WHEEL.
WEST SEDONA
TO COTTONWOOD
89A
ELEV. 4400'
AIRPORT ROAD
0.5 MILES
-LEGEND-
PAVED ROAD
FOOT TRAIL
P PARKING/ TRAILHEAD
VORTEX
START
GUARD RAIL
P
VIEW
ELEV. 4600'
VIEW
VIEW
N
ELEV. 4600'
AIRPORT MESA
SEDONA (OAK CREEK) AIRPORT
VIEW
VIEW
ELEV. 4800'
OAK CREEK
ELEV. 4600'
VIEW
SEDONA

AIRPORT MESA VORTEX LOOP
360° VIEWS FROM MESA RIM TRAIL

DISTANCE: 3.5 MILES
TIME: 2 HOURS
EFFORT: FAIRLY TOUGH
TYPE: LOOP
ROUTE FINDING: EASY
SEASON: SEP to JUN

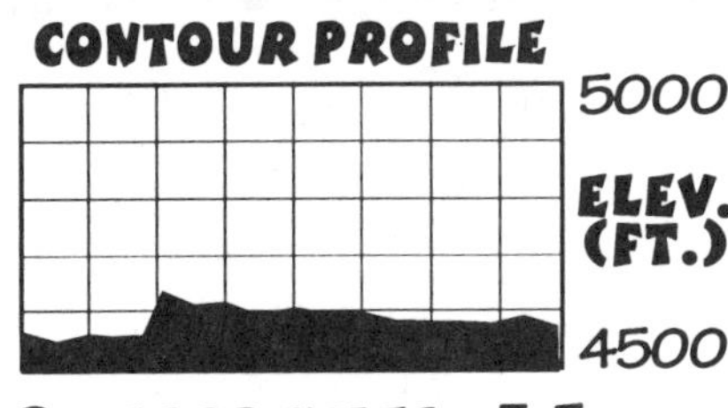

DESCRIPTION: If you're in Sedona and simply *MUST* visit a vortex, but just the thought of physical effort makes you break out in a cold sweat, this is *your* vortex. Call it the lazy man's vortex, the drive-in vortex so to speak. Just pile out of the car, follow the crowd up the short hill and breathe in view and vibe.

VORTEX SITE

However, if you are reading this book, you are most likely the type that loves views, hates crowds and is born to walk. Airport Mesa Trail is right in the heart of Sedona, circumnavigates the rim of Airport Mesa and ends up back at the vortex where you parked the heap. You are high enough off the deck to get great views and as the trail leads you in a big circle you will be able to spy the redrock wonders of Sedona in *every* direction. There is nothing you cannot see from this trail.

Although there is only one short bit of vertical gain that switchbacks up after about a mile, the trail is fairly level. However, oh mother, is it rocky. Chunks of busted basalt embedded in the soil make this a boot hike and a tough one at that. Save the vortex visit for the end of your hike. You end up there anyway in about 2 hours.

DIRECTIONS: Easy to find. From the "Y" junction of HWY 89A and HWY 179 in Sedona head west on HWY 89A for 1 mile toward West Sedona. Go LEFT on Airport Road. The vortex parking lot will be on your left another 0.5 miles up the hill. The whole area will be crawling with tourists. The hike begins behind the guardrail across the road from the vortex parking lot just a few feet uphill of the lot. Bring binocs, water, snack and hat.

BEAR MOUNTAIN

BEAR MOUNTAIN TRAIL
STRENUOUS CLIMB TO EPIC VIEWS

DISTANCE: 6 MILES
TIME: 4 to 5 HOURS
EFFORT: HARD
TYPE: OUT & BACK
ROUTE FINDING: EASY
SEASON: ALL YEAR
(really hot in summer)

CONTOUR PROFILE

6300
ELEV. (FT.)
4600
0 1-WAY MILES 3

DESCRIPTION: From a great distance, Bear Mountain does or does not look like the silhouette of a bear depending on what you've been drinking the night previous. Nor is the summit even visible at the trailhead. However, the views from Bear Mountain are jaw-dropping. You'll especially enjoy the hoodoos, natural columns of rock protected by a capstone which take on fantastic shapes. Surrender to your imagination!

Bear Mountain Trail consists of four levels or steps plus summit, each revealing the next. Begin with a meander across a series of deep washes then head steeply up the first step. Follow cairns scrupulously and avoid any false trail leading up an inviting wash.

Steps 2, 3 and 4 each present stunning views of gnarled hoodoos, adjacent canyons, spires and vast expanses. The trail turns Rambo-esque as the last not-for-fraidy-cats push to the summit ascends a huge tilted slickrock face. Total gain is 1700 feet.

Finally on top you get the prize, a view north to Secret Mountain Wilderness and the San Francisco Peaks way way beyond. Turn around and you get the Sedona *big picture* to the east, south and west.

DIRECTIONS: Easy to find. From the "Y" in Sedona follow my map to Dry Creek Road and then on to newly paved Boynton Pass Road FS 152C . The trailhead parking lot (shared with Doe Mountain Trail) is on the left and directly across the road from Bear Mountain Trail.

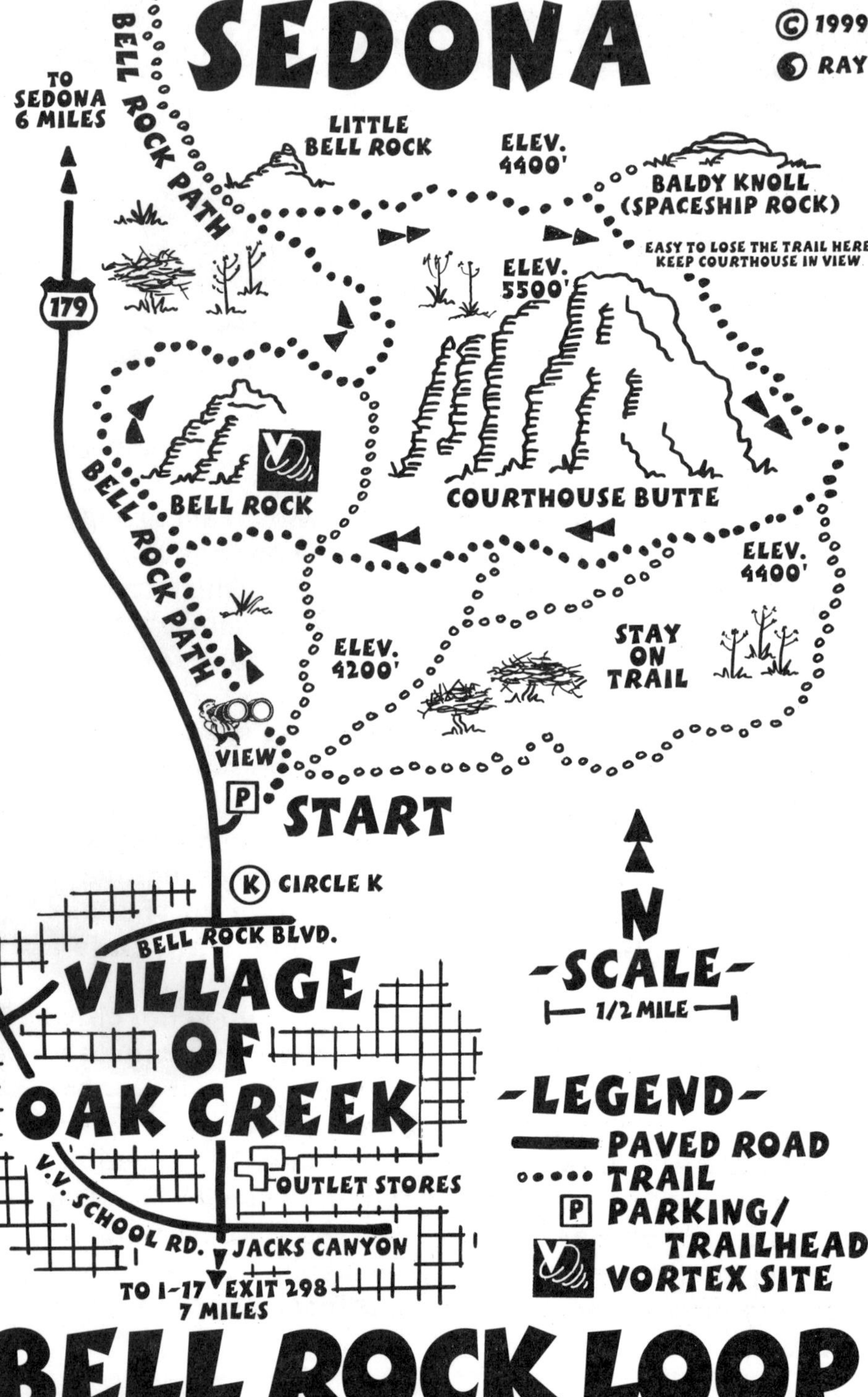
SEDONA
© 1999
RAY
TO SEDONA 6 MILES
BELL ROCK PATH
LITTLE BELL ROCK
ELEV. 4400'
BALDY KNOLL (SPACESHIP ROCK)
EASY TO LOSE THE TRAIL HERE KEEP COURTHOUSE IN VIEW
179
ELEV. 5500'
BELL ROCK
COURTHOUSE BUTTE
BELL ROCK PATH
ELEV. 4400'
ELEV. 4200'
STAY ON TRAIL
VIEW
P
START
K CIRCLE K
BELL ROCK BLVD.
VILLAGE OF OAK CREEK
N
-SCALE-
1/2 MILE
-LEGEND-
PAVED ROAD
TRAIL
P PARKING/ TRAILHEAD
VORTEX SITE
OUTLET STORES
V.V. SCHOOL RD.
JACKS CANYON
TO I-17 EXIT 298 7 MILES
BELL ROCK LOOP

BELL ROCK LOOP
SCENIC MONUMENT LOOP TRAIL

DISTANCE: 4.8 MILES
TIME: 2.0 to 2.5 HOURS
EFFORT: MODERATE
TYPE: LOOP
FIND ROUTE: MODERATE
SEASON: SEP to MAY

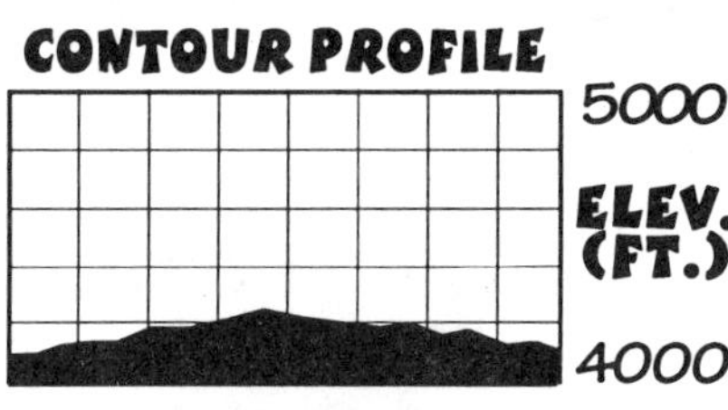

DESCRIPTION: Easy to circle two of Sedona's most spectacular and well known towering red rock monuments. Bell Rock has a characteristic bell shape with it's top looking like a craggy face staring skyward. Bell is a well known masculine vortex site said to boost both physical and spiritual energy. Bulky Courthouse lacks such a distinctive shape, but is a red stone beauty nonetheless because of the way the sun and shadows play across its radiant crimson sandstone fissures and features.

VORTEX SITE

START at parking area/trailhead a few yards north of the Circle K mini-mart in Village of Oak Creek. Follow Bell Rock Path toward Bell. The wide path is easy to follow and leads up, around and behind Bell. About 100 yards before Little Bell Rock a trail leads off to the right. A sign marks the turn. Do not follow any trail heading up toward the top of Bell, but rather follow along its contour. The monuments are always in sight. In this way, you won't get lost. Cairns mark way, but are unreliable.

DIRECTIONS: Find the Village of Oak Creek 6 miles south of Sedona on HWY 179. Now find the Circle K. Easy as pie. There's a killer bakery in The Village for tasty treats and a supermarket near the corner of Verde Valley School Road and HWY 179 .

SEDONA

TO SEDONA 15 MI.
179
TO PHOENIX 100 MI.
TO FLAGSTAFF 40 MI.
17
EXIT 298
2.0 MILES
COCONINO NATIONAL FOREST
-LEGEND-
PAVED ROAD
DIRT ROAD
TRAIL
T TRAILHEAD/ PARKING
N
SCALE
1 MILE
START
RANGER STATION (NO SERVICES)
WET BEAVER CREEK
BELL TRAIL
APACHE MAID TRAIL
GAUGING STATION
WEIR TRAIL
BELL CROSSING
BELL TRAIL
BELL TRAIL
(WET BEAVER CREEK)

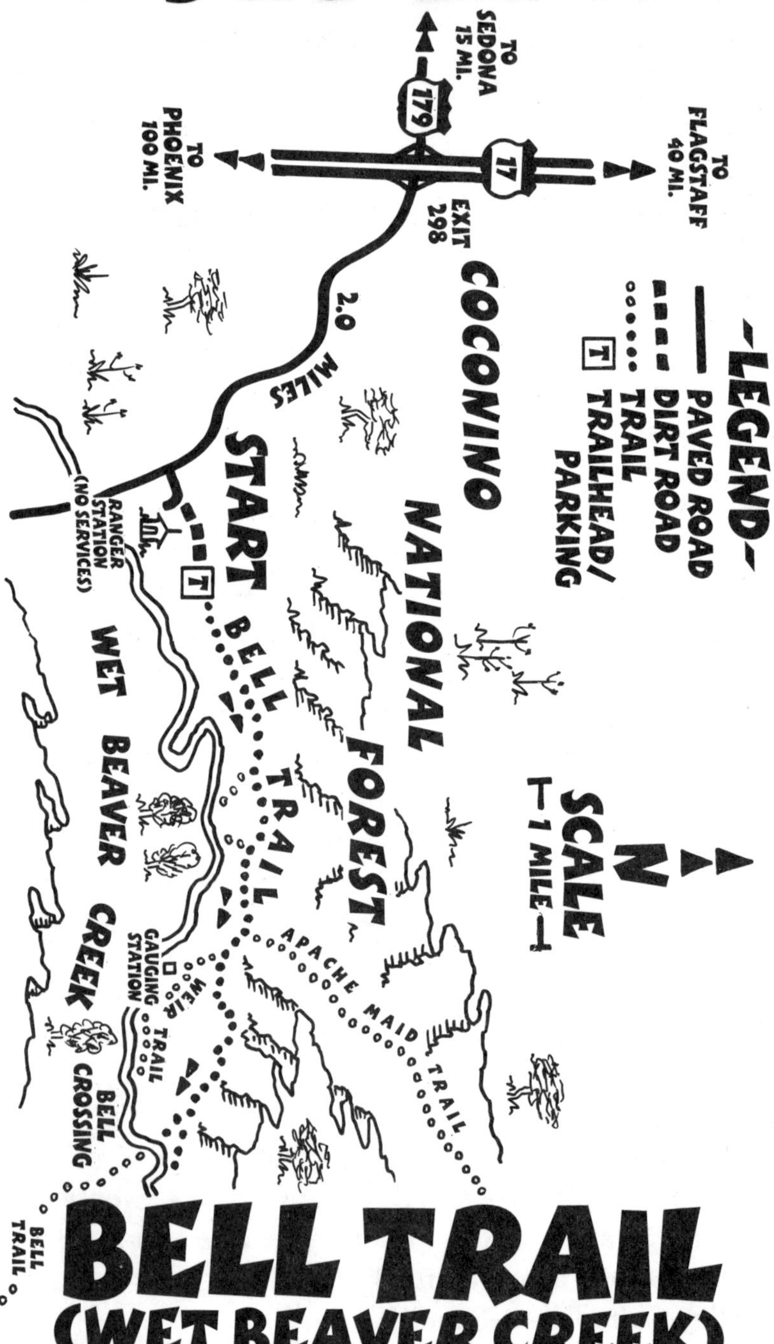

BELL TRAIL
EASY HIKE ALONG BEAVER CREEK

DISTANCE: 8 MILES
TIME: 3 to 4 HOURS
EFFORT: MODERATE
TYPE: OUT & BACK
ROUTE FINDING: EASY
SEASON: ALL YEAR

DESCRIPTION: Water running clear and clean with deep pools and redrock cliffs for diving sounds like just the ticket when that Arizona sun gets cranking. There is a fairly easy trail to just such a magic spot at Bell's Crossing with several spurs along the way to access and enjoy Wet Beaver Creek.

Bell Trail was built by Charlie Bell in the 1930s to run his hungry cattle up to summer pasture on the Mogollon Rim. Never did he envision so many humans with a hunger to calm their souls by the side of his creek. Weekends bring crowds. It's better off-season or during the week.

As you leave the parking lot, the trail is wide and smooth, but runs through private property. You must go about a quarter mile on the trail before you can drop down to the creek. Bell Trail continues on easy rolling terrain until you have gone about three miles. Then you go up and over high above the creek. Finally, Bell drops down to Beaver Creek at the cliffs, ledges and pools of Bell's Crossing. From there Bell Trail crosses Beaver Creek and climbs 1,000 dry and rocky vertical feet to the rim.

Always use caution when diving. Look before you leap. There are no public services at the ranger station. You'll find a formal campground near the ranger station and there are a few wilderness creekside spots just below the gauging station off the Weir Trail.

DIRECTIONS: Bell Trail and Wet Beaver Creek are just off I-17 and way easy to find. Take exit 298 where I-17 meets HWY 179 about 15 miles south of Sedona. Follow the signs to the parking area about 2 paved miles east.

"Beware of enterprises that require new clothes."
- Henry David Thoreau

BOYNTON CANYON

-LEGEND-

PAVED ROAD
TRAIL
152 FOREST ROAD
P PARKING/TRAILHEAD
V VORTEX

N

NOT TO
-SCALE-

SECRET
MOUNTAIN
WILDERNESS

ELEV.
5100'

BOYNTON
SPIRES

VISTA TRAIL

ENCHANTMENT
RESORT
(PRIVATE)

START

ELEV.
4600'

0.25 MI

1.6 MILES

152 C

TO
LONG
CANYON

TO
BOYNTON
PASS

152 C
BOYNTON PASS ROAD

TO
VULTEE
ARCH

TO
FLAGSTAFF

152 C

2.9 MILES

152

DRY CREEK ROAD 152

89A

THE
"Y"

89A

MILE
POST
371

3.1 MILES

179

TO
COTTONWOOD

TO
VILLAGE
OF
OAK CREEK
& I-17

SEDONA

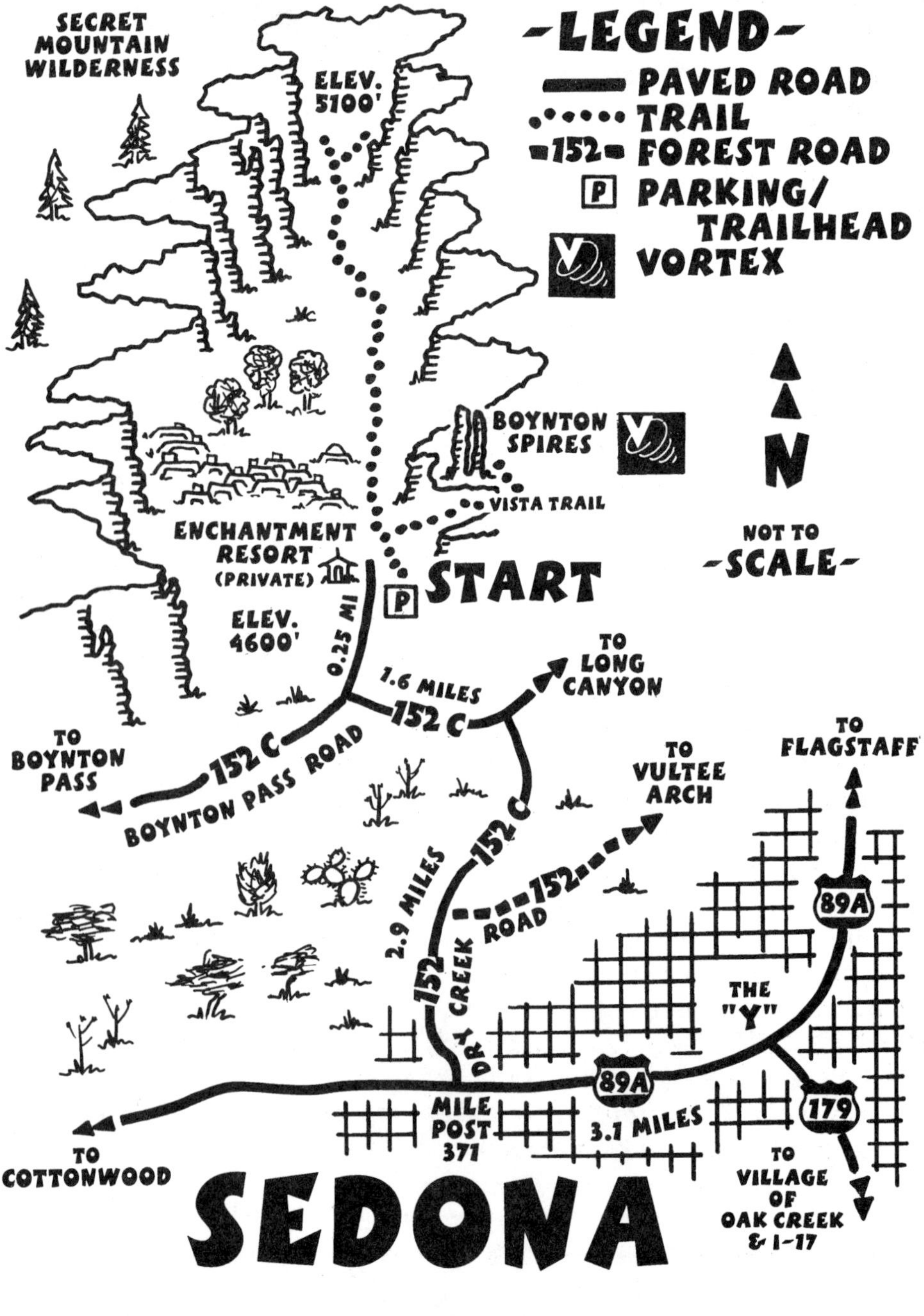

BOYNTON CANYON TRAIL
EASY RAMBLE UP A SCENIC CANYON

DISTANCE: 3 MILES
TIME: 1 to 2 HOURS
EFFORT: EASY
TYPE: OUT & BACK
ROUTE FINDING: EASY
SEASON: ALL YEAR

DESCRIPTION: This scenic and most visited box canyon in Sedona is also a vortex site. Ruins dot the red sandstone canyon walls. Towering buttes, crimson cliffs and a quiet trail on the cool canyon floor all add up to magic, vortex or no. And you'll have company here. Locals and tourists of every stripe come to experience this canyon and its vortex. Some expect flying saucers or God knows what. Truth is, just find a quiet spot, calm down, look at the rocks and listen to the wind between your ears. You'll figure it out. This place has a special feeling. Surrender to that feeling.

VORTEX SITE

All of Boynton Canyon is said to be a magnetic vortex, but there is one particular spot that is said to be the focus of this energy. Immediately after leaving the trailhead, Vista Trail forks off right and leads up a short stroll to Boynton Spires where the vortex is said to reside, especially at the foot of the monument/spire known as Kachina Woman. You'll spot her right away.

Enjoy great views and have cautious fun walking around the spires. Boynton Canyon Trail officially ends at 1.3 miles where it appears to cliff out. After that, continue at your own risk.

DIRECTIONS: Paved road all the way to the trailhead. From the "Y" in Sedona head southwest 3.1 miles toward Cottonwood on Highway 89A. Turn right at milepost 371 onto Dry Creek Road. Follow the map to the trailhead parking area . Signs clearly mark the way.

BRIN'S MESA

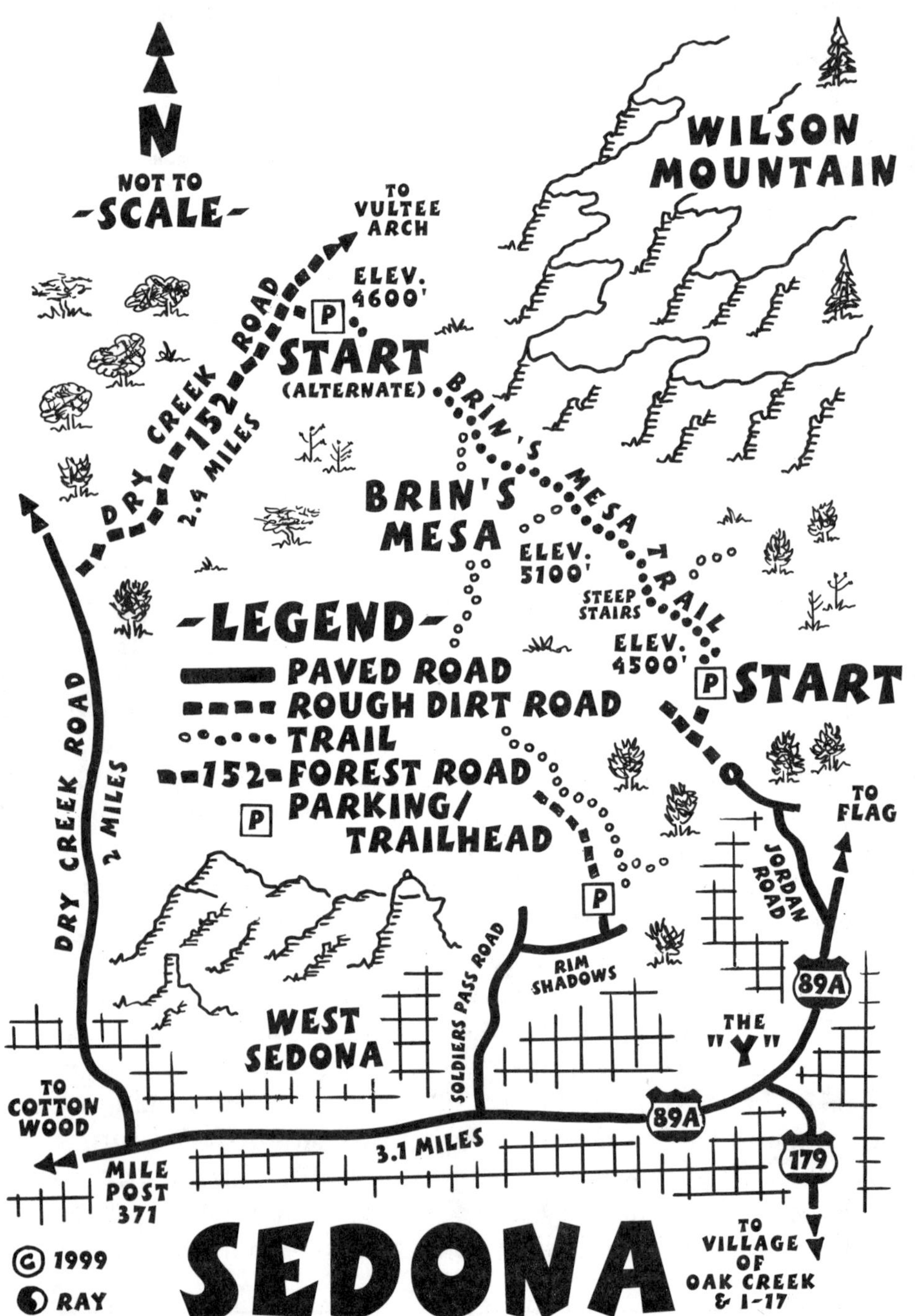

SEDONA

BRINS MESA TRAIL
EASY SCENIC PATH ABOVE SEDONA

DISTANCE: 4.5 MILES
TIME: 2.0 to 2.5 HOURS
EFFORT: MODERATE
TYPE: OUT & BACK
ROUTE FINDING: EASY
SEASON: ALL YEAR

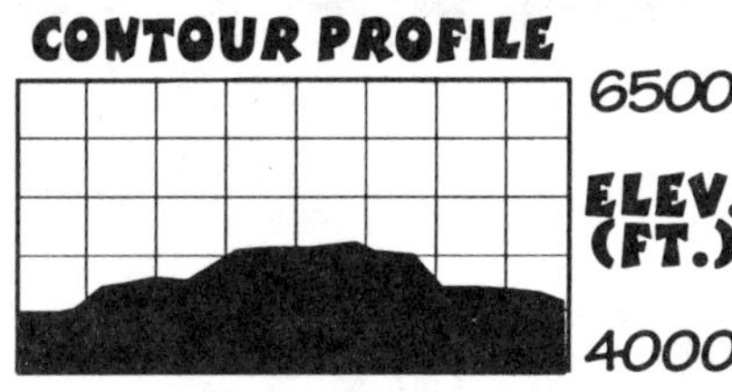

DESCRIPTION: A scenic stroll across an open mesa along the sculpted terracotta base of Wilson Mountain follows the path of a historic jeep road from one side of Sedona to the other. Do-able all year, but quite hot in summer, requiring 2 quarts of water. Brin's Mesa Trail is out in the open and 800 ft. above Sedona offering unobstructed views of surrounding redrock landscape. Brin was an early Sedona settler's brindled bull, hence the name. Simple story, hence no bull.

Brin's Mesa Trail begins right in town at the top of Jordan Road. You may hike an easy out 'n back from either end of the trail or walk the whole way with the help of a shuttle. I like leaving my bike at one end for the return. Heading east to west is slightly tougher because you ascend the mesa via short steep stair steps. The other way is a more gradual climb.

DIRECTIONS: From the "Y" in Sedona go 0.3 miles north on 89A to Jordan Road . Bear left, following the map uphill to a "T" junction. Then left to where the street turns dirt at the end of a paved cul-de-sac. Continue 0.2 mi. to a slick-rock split. Turn right and park. Trailhead is behind gate.

OPTION: Different views, easier climb. Do Brin's Mesa west to east. Begin at the other end from Dry Creek Raod. See the map. From the "Y" go 3.1 miles west to mile-post 371 and go right onto paved Dry Creek Road. After 2 miles turn right onto buttruff (ouch!) F.S.152 Vultee Arch Road. Slow here to keep your and your car's innards intact. Go 2 more miles to marked trailhead on right.

CATHEDRAL ROCK

CATHEDRAL ROCK VORTEX

CATHEDRAL ROCK IS A MAGNETIC VORTEX WHICH BALANCES THE BODY'S ENERGIES AND SUPPLIES A FEELING OF TRANQUILITY. RATHER THAN BEING IN ONE PARTICULAR SPOT, THERE IS A WAVE PATTERN OF MAGNETIC ENERGY WHICH SURROUNDS CATHEDRAL ROCK AND YOU HAVE ONLY TO RELAX AND SURRENDER TO THE FEELING.

-LEGEND-

PAVED ROAD
TRAIL
CAIRNS
PARKING/ TRAILHEAD
CAUTION
VIEW

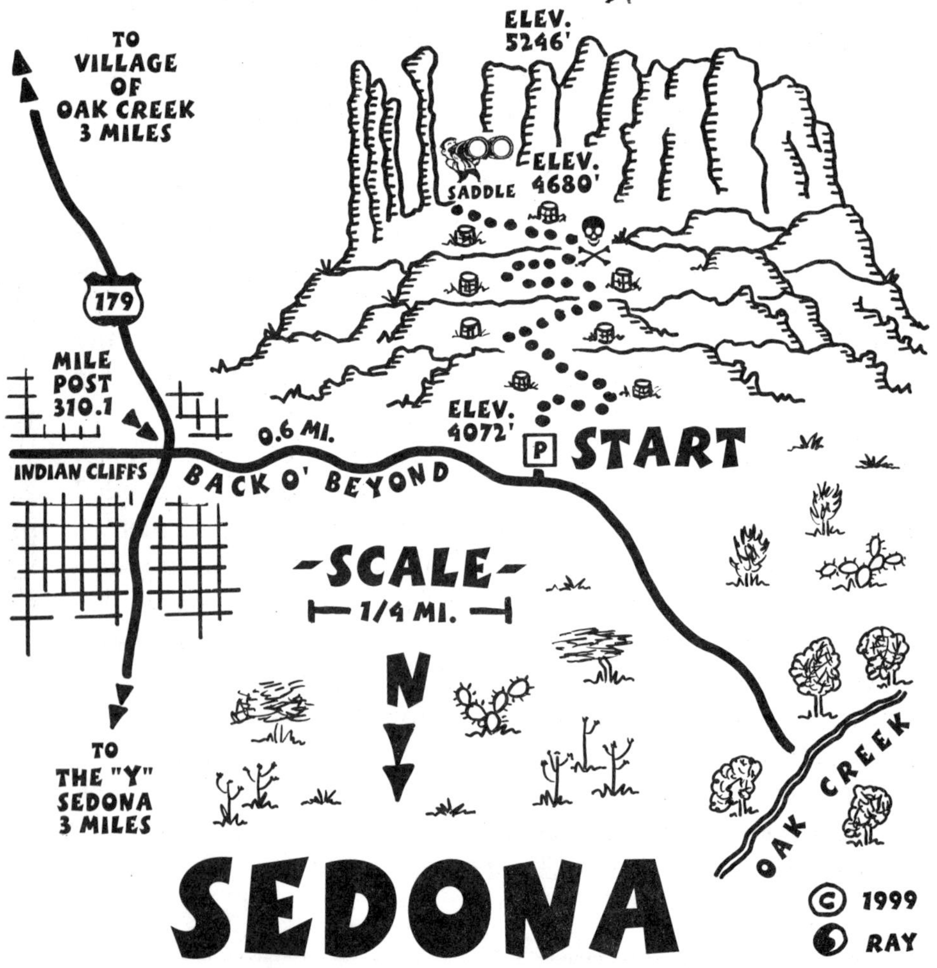

ELEV. 5246'
TO VILLAGE OF OAK CREEK 3 MILES
ELEV. 4680'
SADDLE
179
MILE POST 310.1
0.6 MI.
ELEV. 4072'
P START
INDIAN CLIFFS
BACK O' BEYOND

-SCALE-
1/4 MI.

N

TO THE "Y" SEDONA 3 MILES

OAK CREEK

SEDONA

CATHEDRAL ROCK TRAIL
STEEP & QUICK TO MONUMENTAL VIEW

DISTANCE: 1.4 MILES
TIME: 1 to 1.5 HOURS
EFFORT: MODERATE
TYPE: OUT & BACK
ROUTE FINDING: EASY
SEASON: SEP to JUN

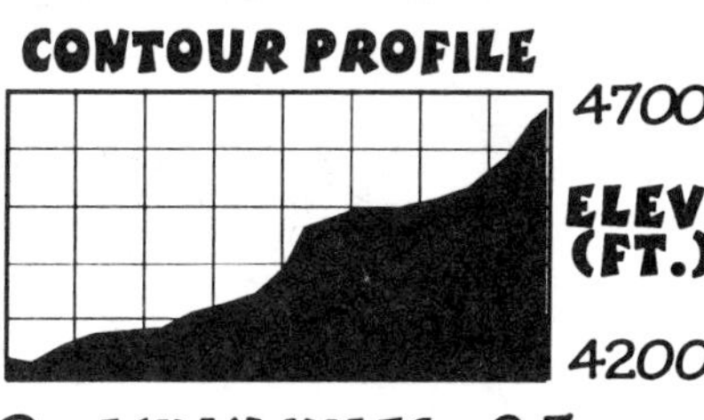

0 **1 WAY MILES** 0.7

DESCRIPTION: Cathedral is Sedona's most photogenic attraction. A well marked trail jumps 600' in 0.7 miles to a saddle between The Mace and The Cathedral and a killer view to all of Sedona's monuments to the south and west . . . Courthouse, Twin Buttes and The Nuns, Lee Mountain and a rare view of Rabbit Ears. This is a favorite short hike and it's a vortex site as well!

VORTEX SITE

The trail easily climbs the platform at the base of Cathedral, but quickly turns steep on a slickrock face. NOT FOR SMALL CHILDREN OR SERIOUS FRAIDY CATS! The trail is super well marked by stones in a series of wire baskets known as cairns. Follow cairns scrupulously and you will be well protected all the way up. Where the slickrock gets steep, there are even stairs carved in the rock. If you lose the trail, go back to the last cairn you saw. Stay on the trail. Although it looks inviting, you can quickly get in over your head on the slickrock.

Avoid cross-country travel. Footprints crush very fragile, small desert plants. Also, desert soil is held together against erosion by a web of bacteria and other microscopic life. A shoeprint may take 10 years to erase. A great deal of effort has been taken to construct this trail so many people can enjoy this fragile environment.

DIRECTIONS: From the "Y" in Sedona head south on HWY 179 to a road with the picturesque name of *Back O' Beyond* at milepost 310.1. Go down *Back O' Beyond* 0.6 miles to the well marked trailhead on your left. A sign warns you to lock your car with valuables out of sight.

COCKSCOMB

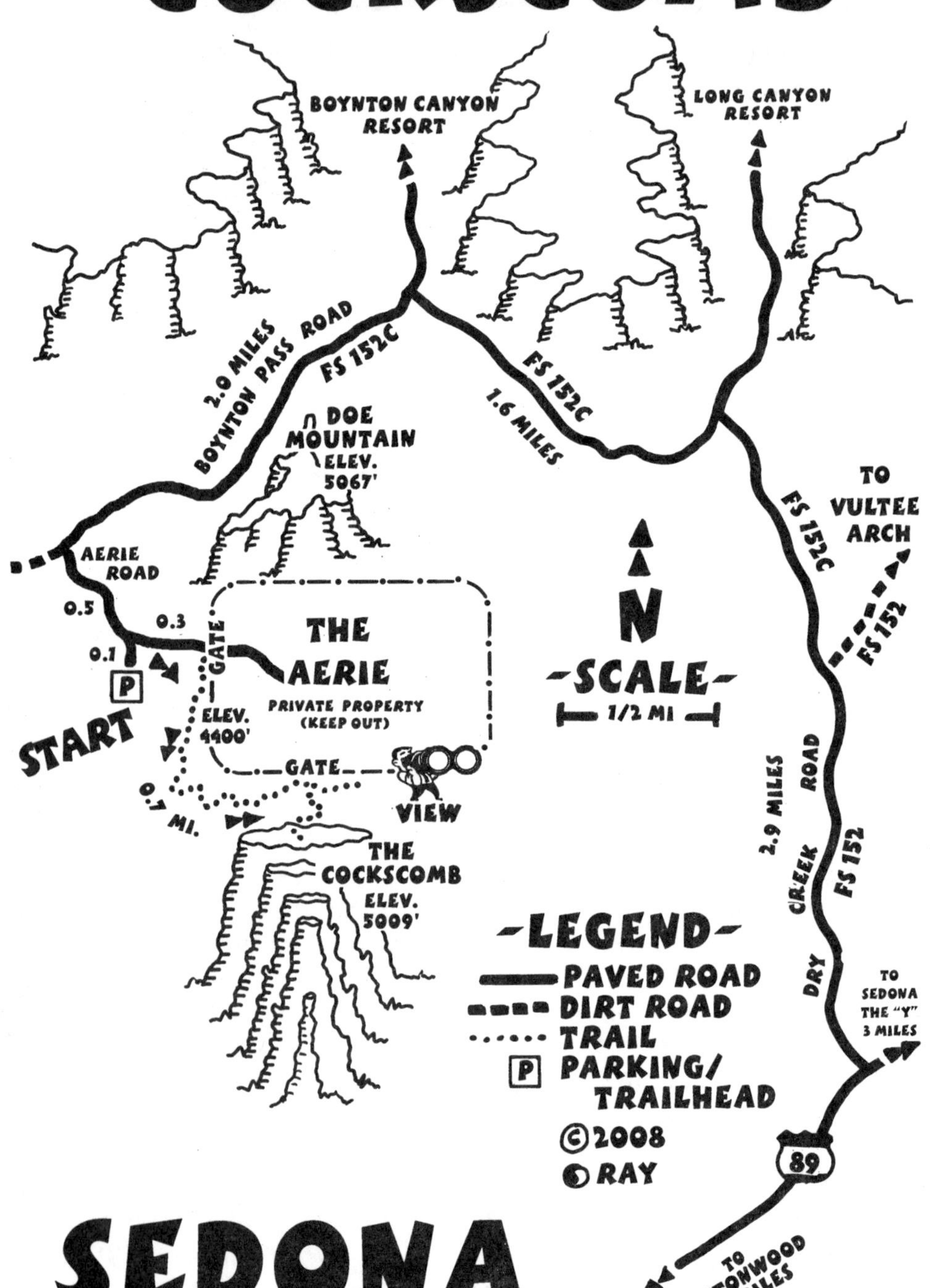

SEDONA

THE COCKSCOMB
HIKE & CLIMB TO A SUPERB PANORAMA

DISTANCE: 1.8 MILES
TIME: 2 TO 3 HOURS
EFFORT: MODERATE
(TOUGH NEAR THE TOP)
TYPE: OUT & BACK
FIND ROUTE: SKETCHY
SEASON: ALL YEAR
(VERY HOT IN SUMMER)

CONTOUR PROFILE

ELEV. (FT.): 4400 – 5009

1-WAY MILES: 0 – 0.9

DESCRIPTION: Are you ready to scale a Sedona red rock monument and top out on a small platform 600 ft. above the deck? Be warned . . . this hike is do-able by fit hikers of steady nerve only, but rewards with great 360° aerial views of Sedona and every direction beyond. The way may be hard to find near the top, requiring a short scramble up a crack in the rim. Remember, there *IS* indeed a route. If it does not look like a trail, it is not. Pay attention so you can find that crack, return the way you came and live to tell the tale.

The spires stick up like the comb of a ginormous rooster in plain view straight ahead as you drive west through Sedona. An informal cairn marked "route" heads up a "non-system" trail to the very top. No technical climbing, but some hand-over-hand work and route finding skill required near the top. Remember, if it does not look like a trail, it probably is not. A mistake can be fatal. Carry food, water and protection from the sun.

The lower trail is darn easy to find and follow albeit unmarked. From the parking lot (see map), walk up the paved road to the entrance to The Aerie (a dwelling or nest on a height) development. The unmarked trail begins just to the right of the gated entrance and runs along the fenceline on public land *OUTSIDE* the private property. After 0.7 miles you arrive at the base of The Cockscomb. Look for the informal cairns that lead up.

DIRECTIONS: The drive is all paved. From the "Y" in Sedona, go west on 89A for 3.1 miles to Dry Creek Road. Note The Cockscomb as you drive out Dry Creek Road. Follow the map. Continue onto Boynton Pass Road FS 152C to Aerie Road. Go LEFT another 0.5 miles. The road splits. Go RIGHT into the parking lot. From there, walk the 0.4 miles back up the paved road to the unmarked trailhead at the entrance to The Aerie. Park in the lower parking lot only. No parking near The Aerie gate.

DEVIL'S BRIDGE

N

NOT TO
-SCALE-

-LEGEND-

PAVED ROAD
BUMPY DIRT ROAD
FOOT TRAIL
152 FOREST ROAD
P PARKING/
TRAILHEAD
PANORAMIC VIEW

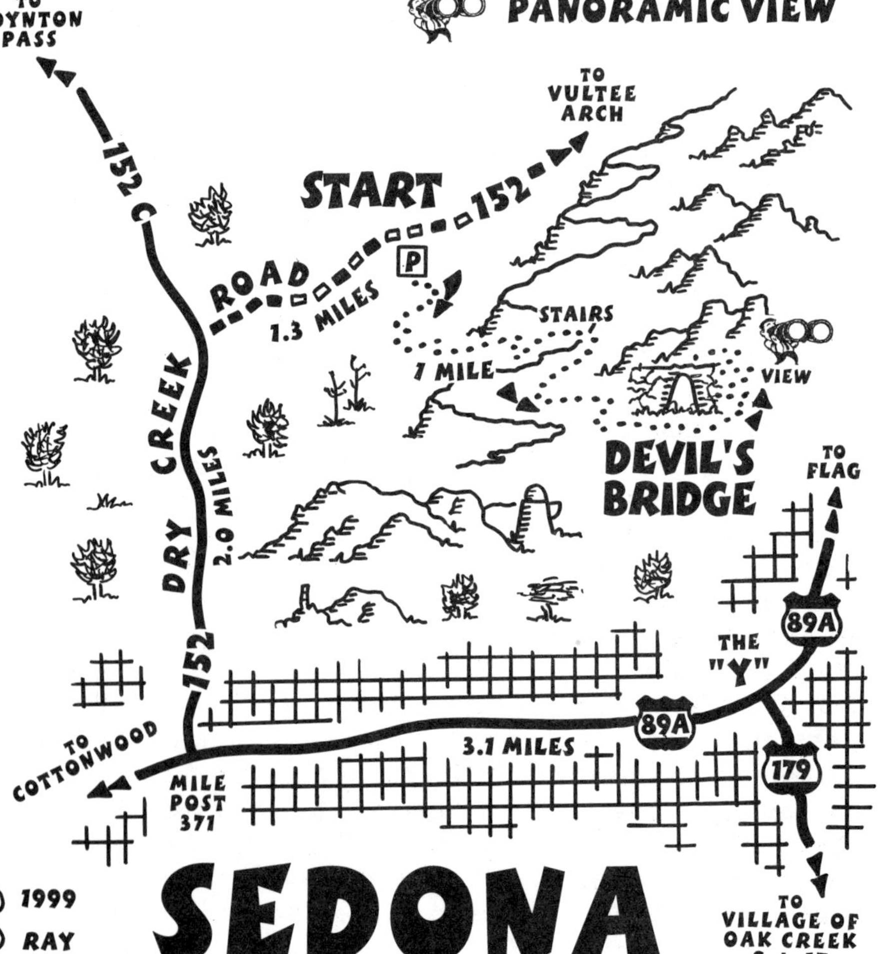

DEVIL'S BRIDGE
EASY WALK TO NATURAL ARCH & VIEW

DISTANCE: 2 MILES
TIME: 1.5 HOURS
EFFORT: FAIRLY EASY
TYPE: OUT & BACK
FIND ROUTE: EASY
SEASON: ALL YEAR

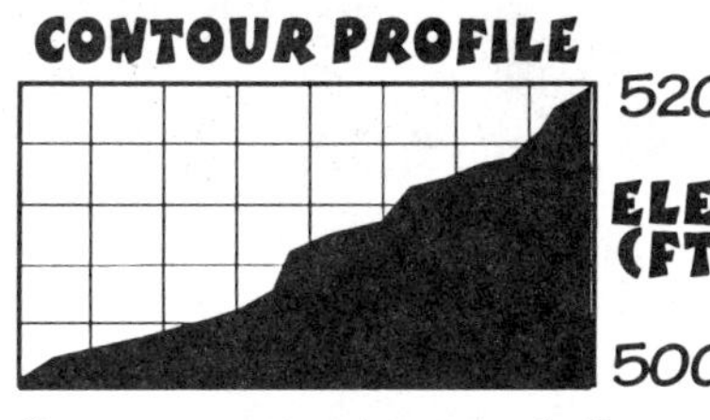

DESCRIPTION: Devil's Bridge is an easy out n' back stroll to what is arguably the most beautiful natural arch in Sedona. It sure gets my vote. The trail is wide and smooth for the most part, but there is a short scramble up some natural stairs as the trail gets a little steep just before the bridge.

The span itself is an ancient, lichen covered, rickety bonzai sculpture with miniature trees and roots growing out of its many photogenic fissures and cracks. It looks as though it may last another ten million years or ten minutes. Foolhardy souls may venture out center span for a photo op, but when a noisy helicopter load of tourists comes whump-whumping close overhead the earth trembles and visions of your entrails being ground to bits on the boulders below . . . well, enough said. Enjoy the view.

DIRECTIONS: From the "Y" in Sedona, head west on Highway 89A 3.1 miles to milepost 371. Go right onto paved Dry Creek Road 2 miles to rough dirt road F.S.152. Go right again 1.3 miles to the well signed trailhead parking area. You'll find F.S. 152 rough as a cob, but can be negotiated easily by cars, especially rental cars, at low speed. You can't see the bridge until you are almost right there, but the Devil's Bridge Trail is signed, well used and well worn, so very little route finding is needed.

DOE MOUNTAIN

SEDONA

DOE MOUNTAIN

CLIMB SKY ISLAND TO VAST PANORAMA

DISTANCE: 3.6 MILES
TIME: 2 TO 3 HOURS
EFFORT: MODERATE
TYPE: OUT & BACK
FIND ROUTE: EASY
SEASON: ALL YEAR

CONTOUR PROFILE

DESCRIPTION: Few climbs to world class views have the virtue of being so easy. Safe, wide and gradual switchbacks snake up the mesa's north side. Doe's flat top is a half mile wide in the east-to-west direction, yet it's narrow waist is only about 200 yards north-to-south, making for easy exploration and navigation.

Since Doe Mountain is covered by a welter of animal trails and tracks and its area so small, you'll find exploration inviting. Watch your step. Use care to minimize your impact by picking a path that will not cause you to break off branches or crush small plants. The mesa's perimeter is entirely paved by nature with large stones making it is possible to rock hop all the way along the rim for 360 degrees of view. Many fine rock outcrops on the island's south side are most suitable for lunch with vast views including most of Sedona's redrock monuments and expanding off into the purple haze many miles distant. Being 400 ft. up, use caution not to become part of the view!

DIRECTIONS: All freshly paved. From the "Y" in Sedona, go west on Highway 89A 3.1 miles to milepost 371, a.k.a. Dry Creek Road. Hang a right onto Dry Creek Road. Follow the map to Boynton Pass Road. Then take a LEFT onto Boynton Pass and continue another 1.2 miles to the trailhead parking lot on the left.

FAY CANYON ARCH

SEDONA

FAY CANYON ARCH

EASY STROLL TO SCENIC ARCH & RUIN

DISTANCE: 1.6 MILES
TIME: 1 HOURS
EFFORT: EASY
TYPE: OUT & BACK
FIND ROUTE: ONE EASY-TO-MISS TURN
SEASON: ALL YEAR

DESCRIPTION: You can't see Fay Canyon Arch from the trailhead. In fact, due to the way it sets right in the face of a blazing terra cotta cliff, you can't see it even when looking right at it. You must hike right up to it. Then you can feel the power of the stresses at work supporting this massive span and you discover it's no illusion. Climb under and around the arch, but explore the ruin with eyes only. Minimize impact. Do not touch the walls or any artifact you may find.

If you know where to look, you'll have no problem spotting the arch. It's massive. Hiking out Fay Canyon Arch Trail, keep an eye on the cliffs to your right. Soon you'll see the form of a huge arc carved high up on the cliff wall. It still won't appear to be an arch, but start looking for possible cairns or an obvious unmarked trail UP after you've gone about 0.5 miles from the trailhead. Most definitely worth the scramble up.

Now leave the tourists behind and explore the rest of this short, hidden canyon which boxes out at a sheer red Supai sandstone cliff with more ancient ruins. Remember, eyes only. Do not touch the ruin.

DIRECTIONS: Easy. From the "Y" in Sedona go west on Highway 89A 3.1 miles to paved Dry Creek Road at mile 371. Go right and follow the map to the trailhead.

HARDING SPRING/ COOKSTOVE LOOP

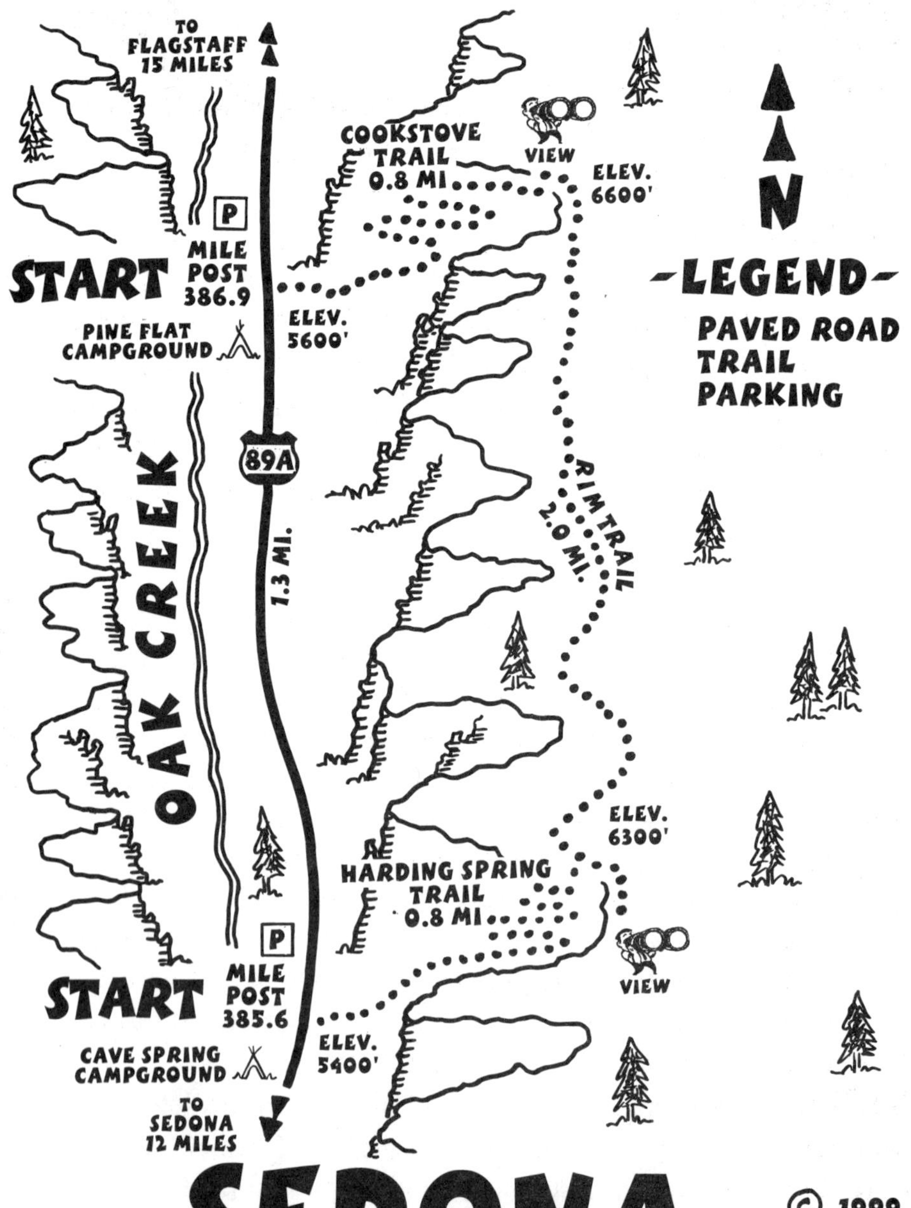

SEDONA

HARDING SPRING/COOKSTOVE
SHORT TOUGH CLIMB TO SUPERB VIEWS

DISTANCE: 4.9 MILES
TIME: 2 to 2.5 HOURS
EFFORT: SHORT & STEEP
TYPE: LOOP
FIND ROUTE: EASY
SEASON: MAR to NOV

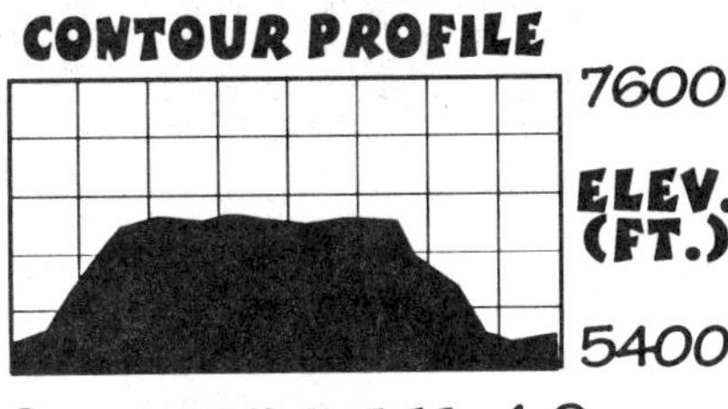

DESCRIPTION: If the truth be told, it's a natural fact that the west side canyon walls of Oak Creek are prettier than the east. Arches, hoodoos, spires and imaginary goblin shapes are sculpted by nature into the buff and terra cotta sandstone cliffs of the west side wall. To see them clearly, you must scale the short, steep wall of the east. Gradual switchbacks up through the cool, shaded forest take some of the sweat out of the climb. Every so often, don't forget to stop, take your eyes off the trail for a moment and watch the kodachrome view develop.

Now follow the rim trail south up and down through a few small washes until you hit the top of Harding Spring Trail. A little side spur walks you out to another great view before you head down to where you dump out back on 89A across from the "Troutdale Ranch" sign at milepost 385.6. The wide shoulder here makes it an easy walk on 89A for the 1.3 miles back to the hiker-mobile or drop down to the creek and pick your way back along the boulders, rushes and beaches. That takes me an extra hour or so. No hurry.

DIRECTIONS: Well marked Cookstove Trail takes off steep up across from a gushing roadside stone fountain at mile 386.9 on Highway 89A, 13 miles north of Sedona or 16 miles south of Flagstaff.

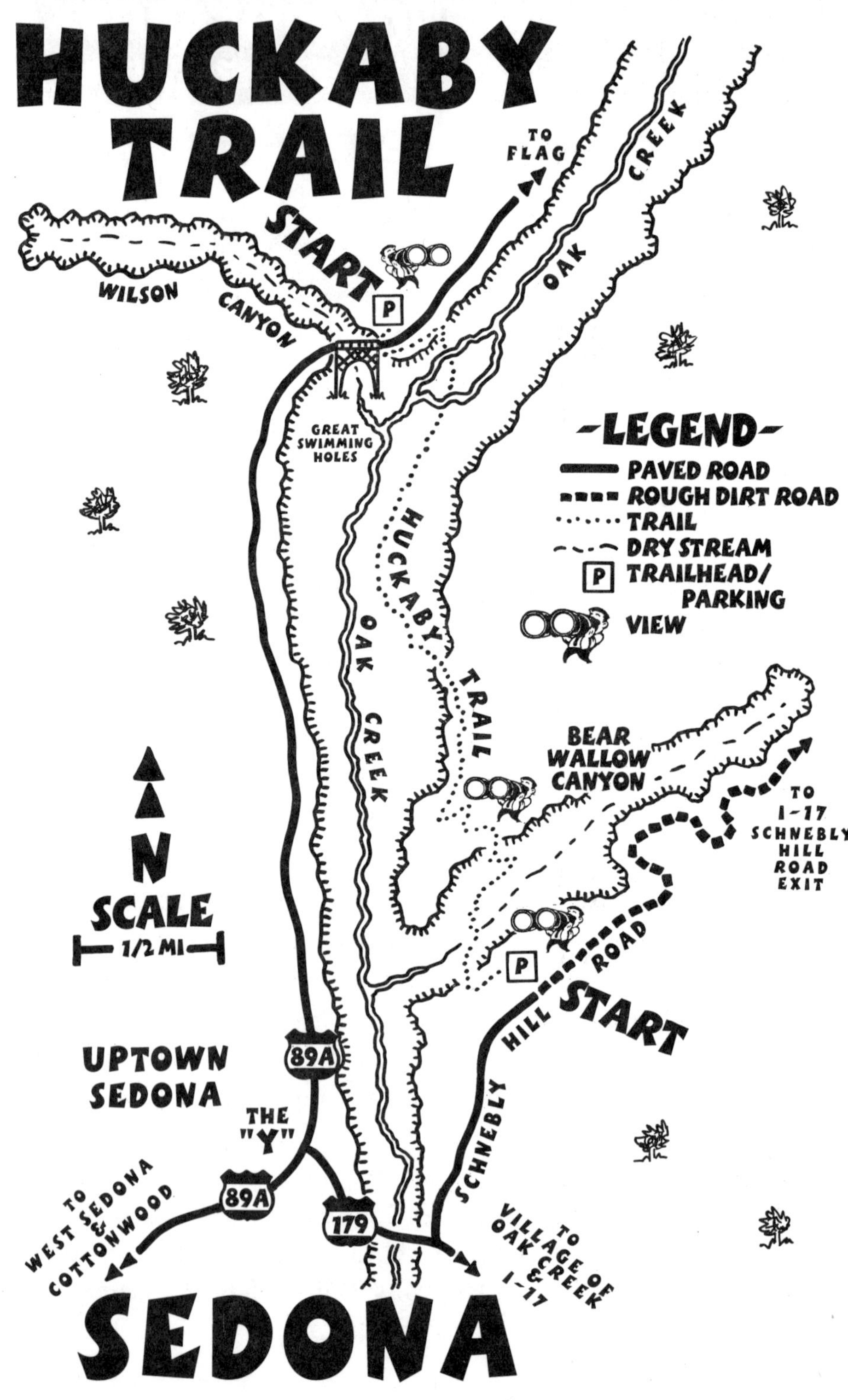
HUCKABY TRAIL
TO FLAG
START
WILSON
CANYON
OAK CREEK
P
GREAT SWIMMING HOLES
HUCKABY TRAIL
OAK CREEK
-LEGEND-
PAVED ROAD
ROUGH DIRT ROAD
TRAIL
DRY STREAM
TRAILHEAD/ PARKING
VIEW
BEAR WALLOW CANYON
TO I-17 SCHNEBLY HILL ROAD EXIT
N
SCALE
1/2 MI
ROAD
START
SCHNEBLY HILL
89A
UPTOWN SEDONA
THE "Y"
89A
179
TO WEST SEDONA & COTTONWOOD
TO VILLAGE OF OAK CREEK & I-17
SEDONA

HUCKABY TRAIL
SECRET OAK CREEK TRAIL WITH VIEWS

DISTANCE: 5 MILES
TIME: 2 TO 3 HOURS
EFFORT: MODERATE
TYPE: OUT & BACK
FINDING: VERY EASY
SEASON: ALL YEAR

AT A GLANCE

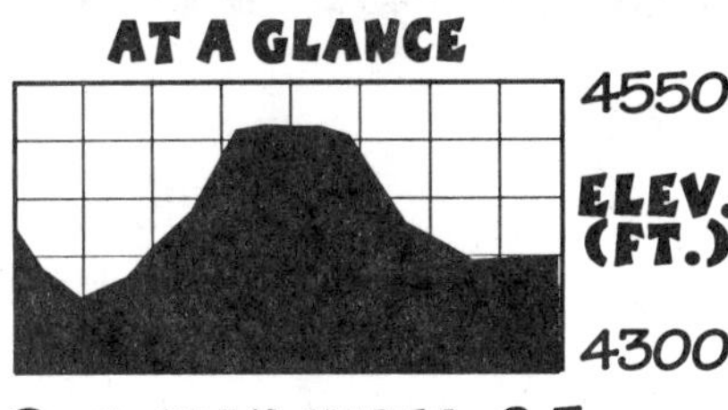

DESCRIPTION: Huckaby Trail traces a scenic route to connect Schnebly Hill Road, secret Oak Creek swimming holes and Midgely Bridge. There are great views of Sedona monuments along the way. You drop into Oak Creek just below Midgely Bridge at a spot that was formerly very hard to access and thus still pretty much a secret.

Huckaby starts from Schnebly Hill Road, dives down into Bear Wallow Canyon, curves around and along the toe of Mitten Ridge as redrock views open up and finally descends to Oak Creek at that secret spot just below Midgely. A great slide/chute style swimming hole is just below the bridge.

OPTIONS: You can also start at Midgely Bridge, although crowded parking can be a problem. The trail begins at the viewing area guardrail under the bridge and leads under the highway and down to the creek.

NOTE: Either way, there is a creek crossing maybe involving rocks and logs. The creek is normally only a foot or so deep, so no big deal if you fall in. Wear your TEVAs and bring a favorite stick. DO NOT ATTEMPT CROSSING OAK CREEK WHEN IT RUNS BIG. YOU COULD DROWN AS IN GLUB, GLUB, GLUB!

DIRECTIONS: From the "Y" junction of HWY 89A and HWY 179 in Sedona, go south on 179 for 0.3 miles. Go left on Schnebly Hill Road 0.7 miles to a parking area on your left. You'll see the sign for Huckaby Trailhead. Do not leave valuables in sight in your car.

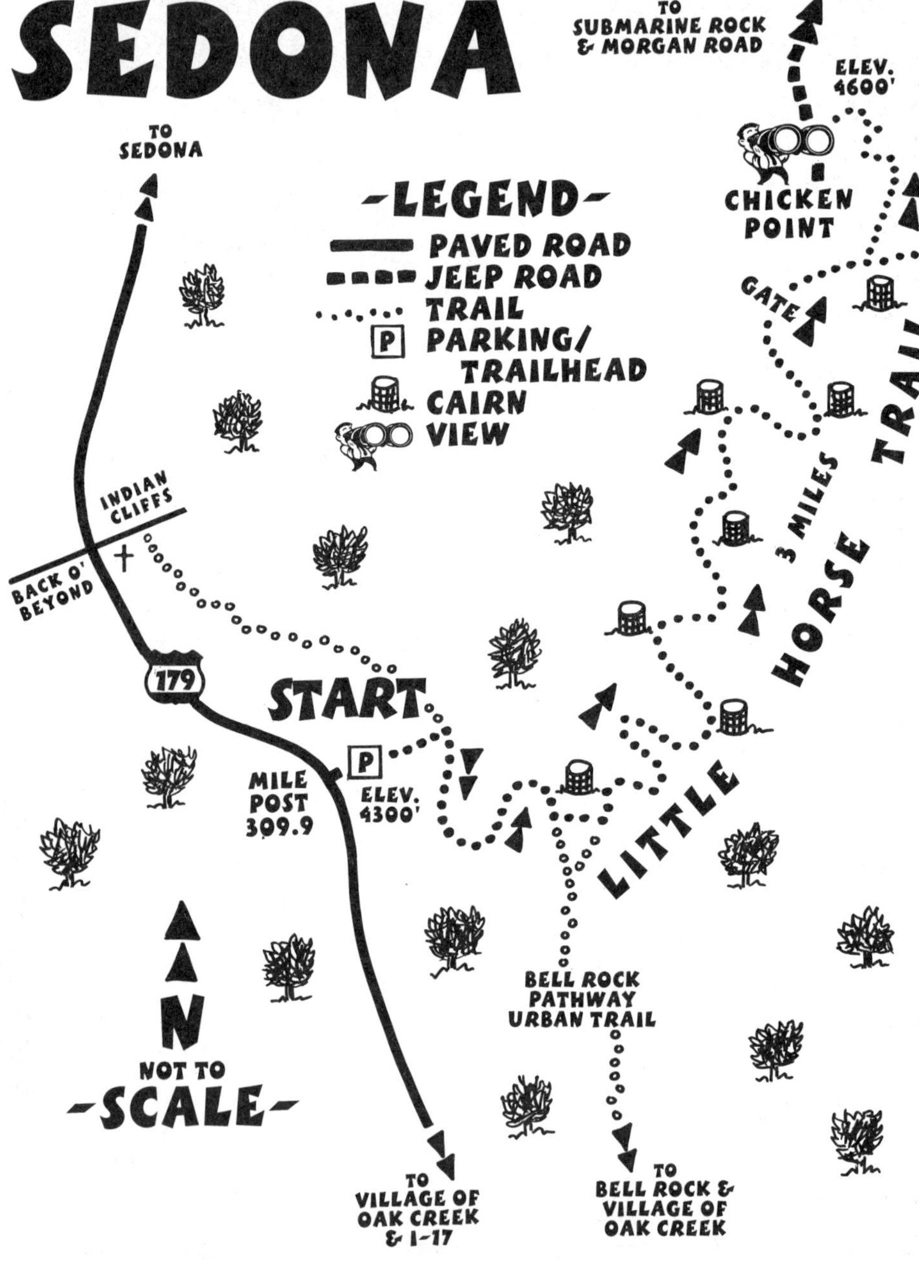

LITTLE HORSE TRAIL

LITTLE HORSE TRAIL
GREAT TRAIL TO VIEWS AND REDROCKS

DISTANCE: 6 MILES
TIME: 2 to 3 HOURS
EFFORT: MODERATE
TYPE: OUT & BACK
FIND ROUTE: EASY
SEASON: SEP TO MAY

DESCRIPTION: Little Horse Trail follows a twisty turny route up through some of Sedona's least known yet most unique redrock formations. Thanks to a great new trailhead and parking area built by the forest service, Little Horse is now easy to find as well. The trail has been greatly improved at the hands of generous volunteer labor over many many hours and is now well marked by a number of bombproof cairns . . . rocks in a wire basket. The result is a natural looking, self guided trail through some of the most beautiful scenery in Sedona.

BEGIN at the new parking area. Head south on the wide Bell Rock Path for about a quarter mile until a sign directs you LEFT up Little Horse Trail. Follow Little Horse for 2 miles until you reach a gate. At the gate, look overhead to your left. You may even hear voices and see people up above. That's Chicken Point. There is a constant flow of jeep peeps and mountain bikers to Chicken Point as it is a favorite view spot. Use the map, follow the bike tracks and find your way up to the great view.

DIRECTIONS: From the "Y" junction of HWY 89A and 179 in Sedona head south on 179 for 3.5 miles to milepost 309.9 and turn into the parking area.

LONG CANYON

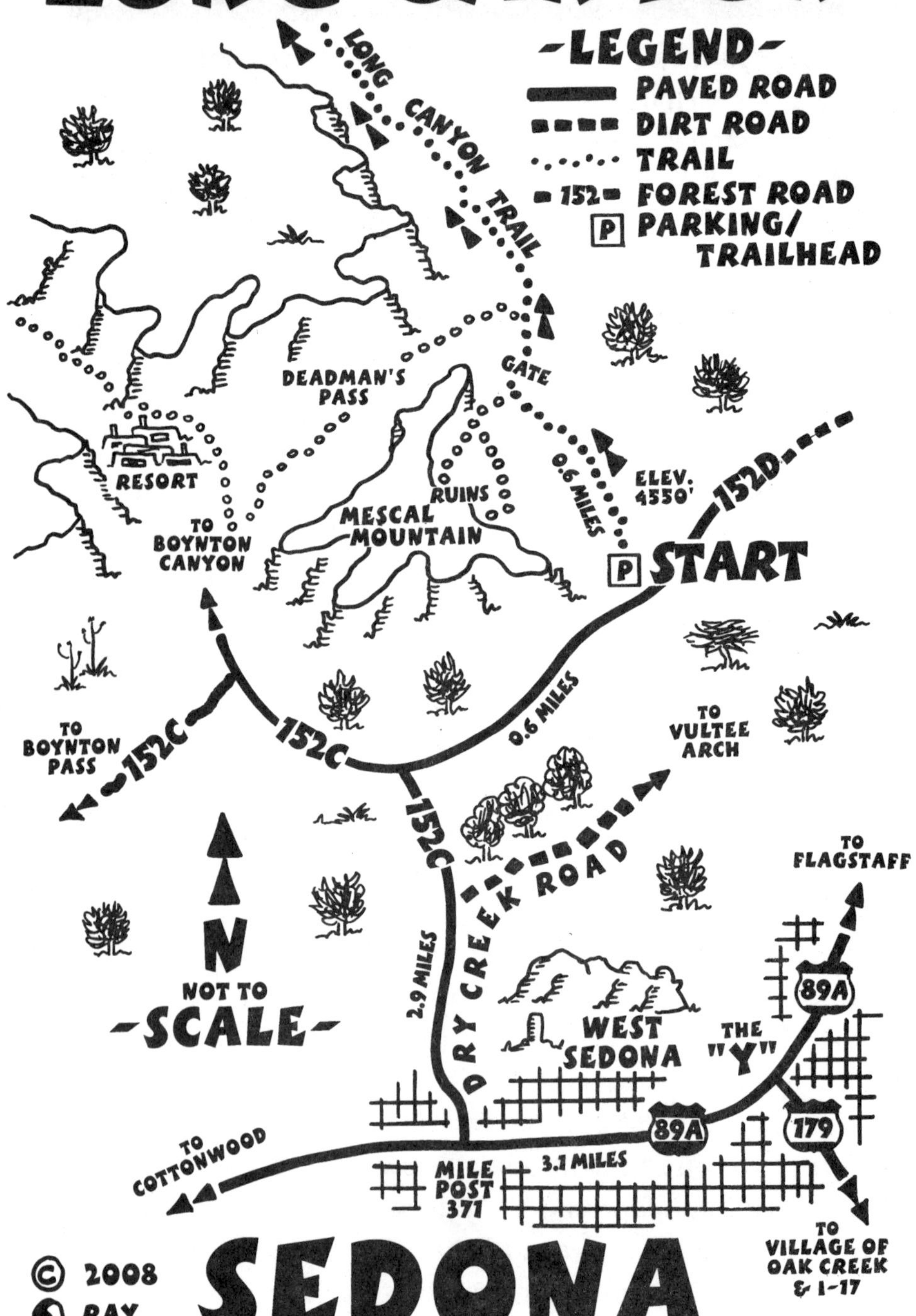

SEDONA

LONG CANYON TRAIL
EASY WALK UP UNIQUE SEDONA CANYON

DISTANCE: 7 MILES
TIME: 2 to 3 HOURS
EFFORT: FAIRLY EASY
TYPE: OUT & BACK
FIND ROUTE: EASY
SEASON: ALL YEAR

DESCRIPTION: As these sedona canyons go, Long Canyon is pretty as any, but with the most boring name. Too bad, because this unique scenic walk sports views of buttes, cliffs, spires, hoodoos, windows and arches for which Sedona is so famous. I jumped a herd of 30 snorting javelina right here. Big as Rottweilers and ready to rumble! These not so gentle, yellow toothed wild boars scared hell out of me as they scattered at first then stood their ground, eyeing me with some suspicion and disdain as well they might.

Humans don't make it back to the end of Long Canyon all that often. Most poop out after a mile or so of this moderate out 'n back and never see the terra cotta hoo-doo formations, stunning redwall cul-de-sac or even the ruins along the sides of Mescal Mountain.

A side stroll just a few hundred meters to the east face of Mescal Mountain (see map) leads to many ruins. Of course, to disturb, touch or rob is a crime, but to snoop around, pause and reflect is a most enlightening Sedona pastime.

DIRECTIONS: All paved roads. From the "Y" in Sedona head west on Highway 89A toward Cottonwood for 3.1 miles to Dry Creek Road at milepost 371. Turn right and go 2.9 miles to Long Canyon Road and turn right again. Go 0.6 miles to the trailhead parking area turnout on your left.

SEDONA
-SCALE-
1/2 MI
-LEGEND-
PAVED ROAD
DIRT ROAD
FOOT TRAIL
T P TRAILHEAD/PARKING
VORTEX SITE
TO WEST SEDONA TRAILS
JIM THOMPSON TRAIL
WILSON MOUNTAIN TRAIL
TO FLAGSTAFF 25 MILES
MIDGLEY BRIDGE
T
OAK CREEK
89A
UPTOWN SEDONA
ELEV. 4400'
TO WEST SEDONA
THE "Y"
SEDONA SPORTS
179
TO V.O.C. & I-17
SOMBART
MARG'S DRAW TRAIL
TO BROKEN ARROW TRAILS
HUCKABY TRAIL
START
N
DAMIFINO TRAIL
BEAR WALLOW CANYON
MUNDS WAGON TRAIL
SCHNEBLY HILL ROAD
THE COW PIES
ELEV. 5000'
SLICKROCK
VIEW
VIEW
ELEV. 5600'
THE CAROUSEL
P
MUNDS WAGON TRAIL
VIEW
SCHNEBLY VISTA
ELEV. 6000'
TO I-17 AT EXIT 320 6 MILES
MUNDS WAGON TRAIL
SCHNEBLY HILL TRAILS
© 2003
RAY

MUNDS WAGON TRAIL
SCENIC HIKE UP TO A HOO-DOO CAROUSEL

DISTANCE: 4 MILES 1-WAY
TIME: 3 to 4 HOURS
EFFORT: STRENUOUS
8 MILE ROUND TRIP
TYPE: OUT & BACK
(LONG LOOP POSSIBLE - SEE MAP)
ROUTE FINDING: EASY
SEASON: ALL YEAR
HIKE EARLY IN SUMMER

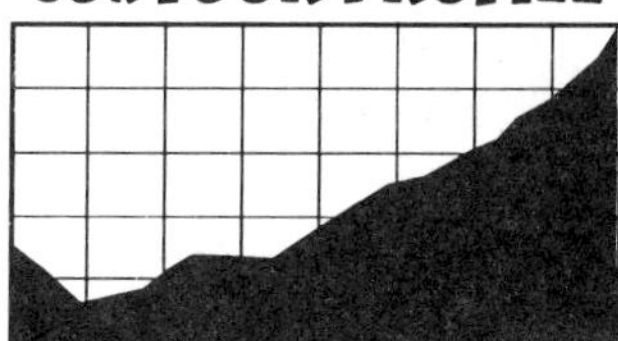

DESCRIPTION: Munds Wagon Trail leads up a storybook canyon to a kodachrome fantasy world of views, monuments, spires, hoo-doos, carousels and even a slickrock vortex.

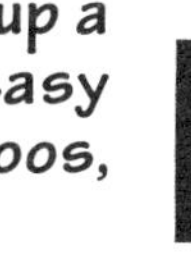

VORTEX SITE

The route begins mostly shaded and ascending up through Bear Wallow Wash. The pools and red stone surfaces of the wash have been scoured and smoothed over the ages by the force of water rushing to Oak Creek. As the trail rises up out of the creekbed, technicolor views expand to the south and west overlooking Sedona and surrounding redrock formations.

After 2.5 miles, a detour off the trail leads onto The Cow Pies, a slickrock formation well known for views and a reputation as a vortex site said to have great calming and recuperative powers. See the map.

Near the top, surrender to your imagination. You arrive at The Carousel, a huge circular formation of monstrous stones and hoo-doos sandwiched between massive layers of red rock creating the illusion of creatures on an enormous merry-go-round.

Next, follow the trail along the edge around The Carousel and up to the end of Munds Wagon Trail before beginning your run back down the hill the way you came.

DIRECTIONS: From the "Y" junction of HWY 89A and HWY 179, head SOUTH on HWY 179 for 0.3 miles across Oak Creek Bridge. Turn LEFT on paved Schnebly Hill Road for 0.8 miles and turn LEFT into the Huckaby-Munds Trailhead parking area just as the pavement ends. Bring sunscreen, a camera, lots of water and snackage to fuel the inner hiker.

"If you don't know where you're going, any road will do."
-George Harrison

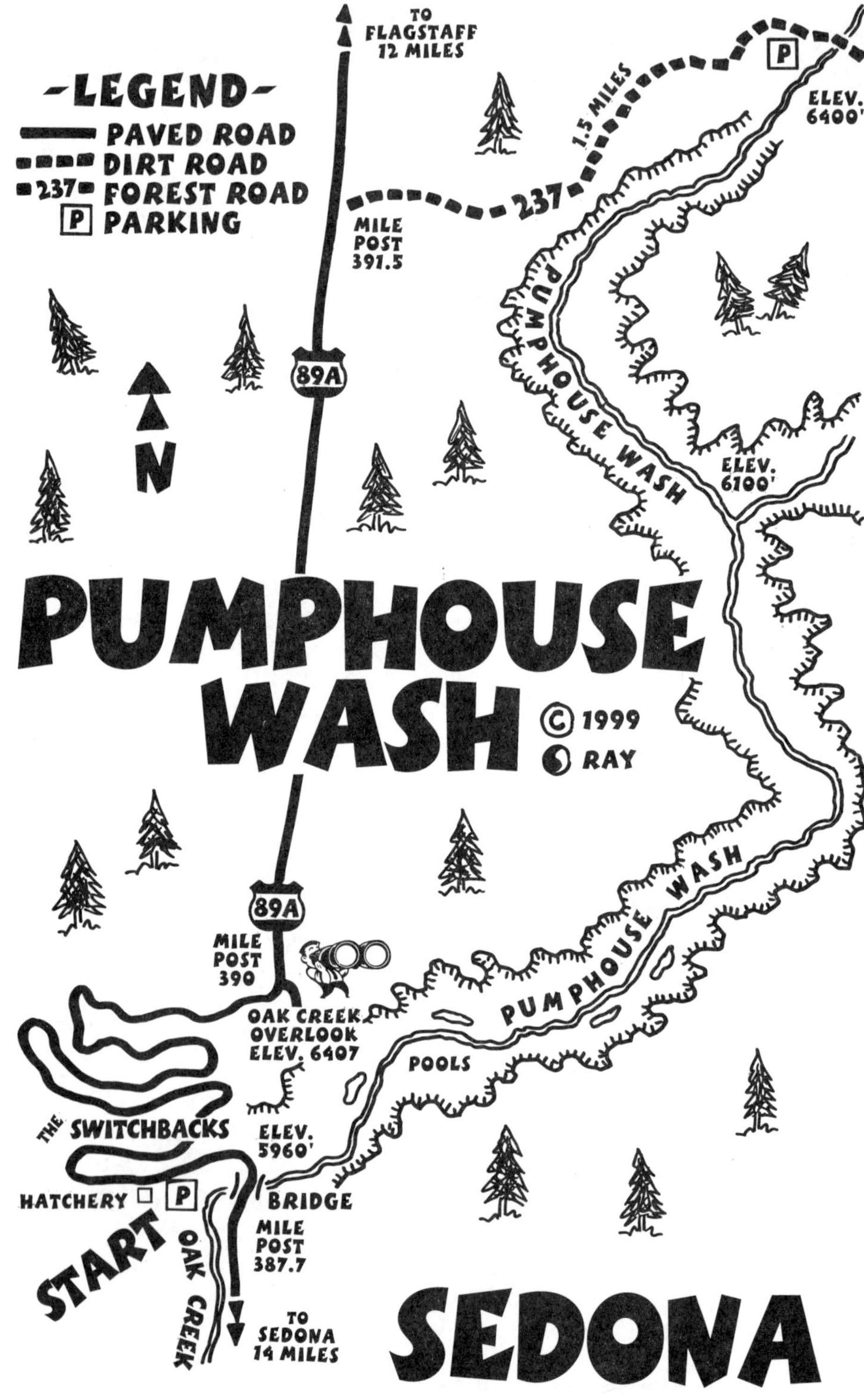
TO
FLAGSTAFF
12 MILES
-LEGEND-
PAVED ROAD
DIRT ROAD
237 FOREST ROAD
P PARKING
1.5 MILES
P
ELEV.
6400'
237
MILE
POST
391.5
PUMPHOUSE WASH
89A
N
ELEV.
6100'
PUMPHOUSE
WASH
© 1999
RAY
PUMPHOUSE WASH
89A
MILE
POST
390
OAK CREEK
OVERLOOK
ELEV. 6407
POOLS
THE SWITCHBACKS
ELEV.
5960'
HATCHERY
P
BRIDGE
START
OAK CREEK
MILE
POST
387.7
TO
SEDONA
14 MILES
SEDONA

PUMPHOUSE WASH

TOUGH BOULDER HOP UP SCENIC WASH

DISTANCE: 2.5 MILES
TIME: 2 to 3 HOURS
EFFORT: DIFFICULT
TYPE: OUT & BACK
FIND ROUTE: EASY
SEASON: ALL YEAR

DESCRIPTION: Boulder bashing at its very best! Not for the feeble, weak, lame, very young or very old. Sad but true. You must be very fit to hop huge boulder to huge boulder for a mile and a quarter up a dry wash and return, but there are rewards. The sculpted red walls of narrow Pumphouse Wash are nearly 1000 ft. high and there are many secluded swimming holes along the way to escape the heat of a Sedona summer day.

I describe an out & back from the bottom of the wash simply because this lower stretch is much more scenic with its steep, sheer cliffs. Plus, the way may be blocked near the bottom of the wash from spring to early summer by deep pools, some 75 ft. long and 30 ft. deep. You must be a competent swimmer or else it's rough to hike 2 miles downstream and have to hike all that way back over rough terrain.

DANGER! Hiking in a deep narrow wash that drains a huge area is a recipe for disaster during summer's July-August afternoon monsoon season. Be aware of where you are and time of day. A high speed wall of water may appear without a cloud in the sky.

DIRECTIONS: From the "Y" in Sedona head north on Highway 89A for 14 miles to the bridge over Pumphouse Wash at milepost 387.7. Park in the wide turnout above the bridge.

SECRET CANYON

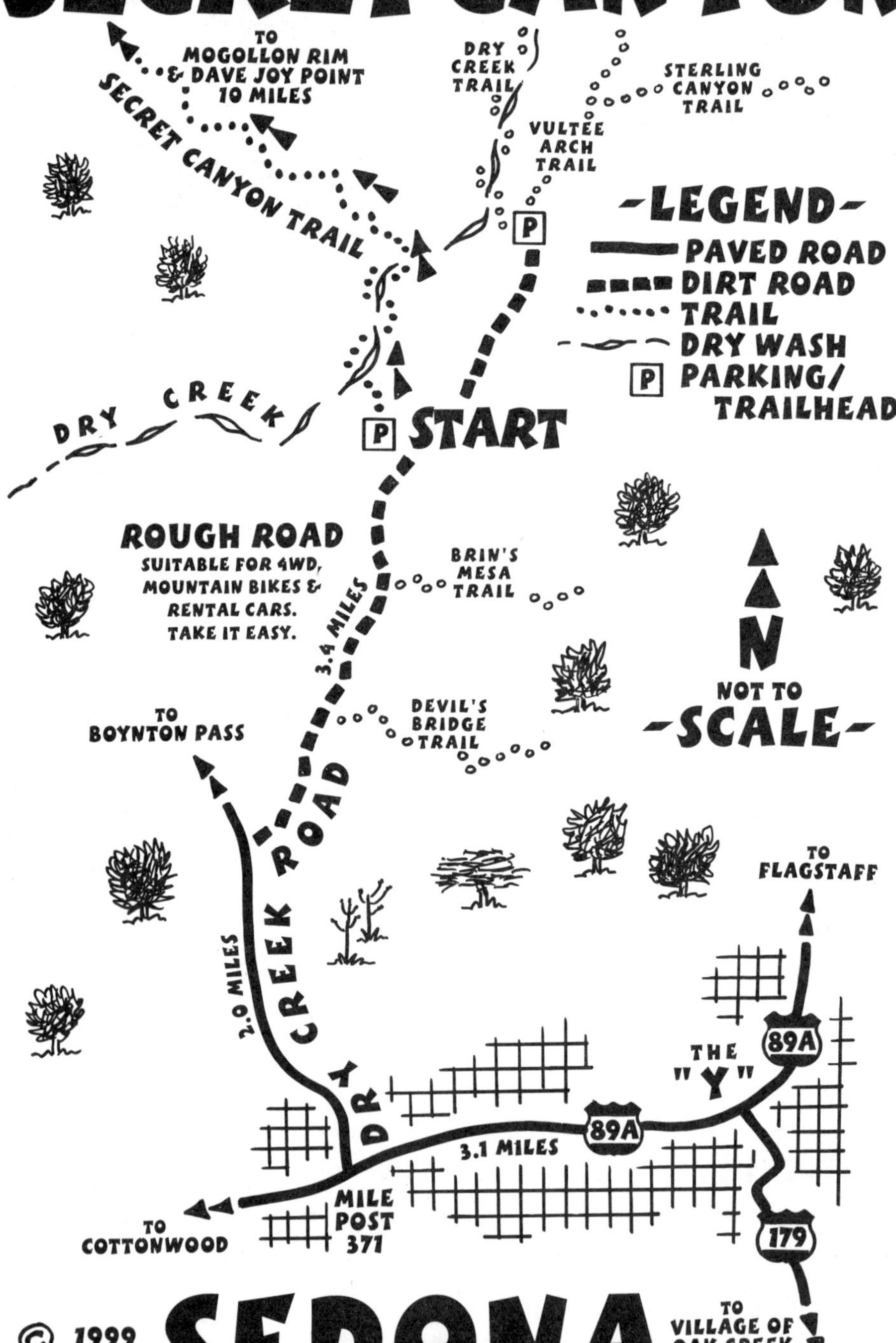

SEDONA

SECRET CANYON
FAVORITE TRAIL UP A REDROCK CANYON

DISTANCE: 6 MILES
TIME: 3 TO 4 HOURS
EFFORT: MODERATE
TYPE: OUT & BACK
FIND ROUTE: EASY
SEASON: ALL YEAR

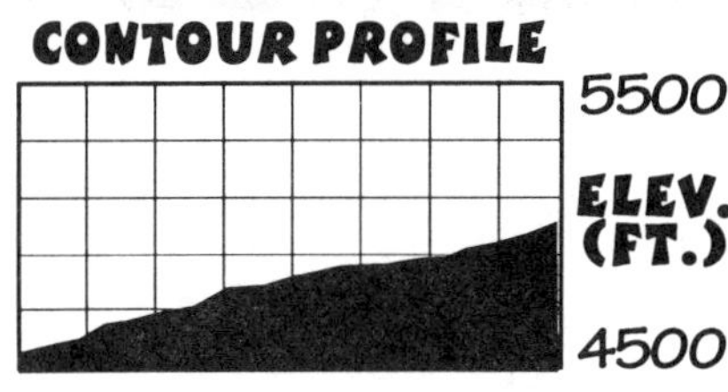

DESCRIPTION: Splashing pools, some really cool redrock formations and easy hiking, but a secret it is not. A big sign on Dry Creek Road announces the trailhead. What kind of a secret is that? Anyway, Secret Canyon is still one of the best scenic creek trails in Northern Arizona.

START this out-and-back at the trailhead parking area 3.4 miles out rough-as-heck dirt Dry Creek Road. The rusty sign in the parking lot reads "Secret Canyon Trail #121". Begin up Dry Creek with three crossings before heading up out of the creekbed. Wear your Tevas in the spring when Dry Creek isn't so dry. These first two miles are out in open pinon and juniper before you enter Secret Canyon. The scenery gets more and more intense as the canyon walls fairly drip with red stone hoodoos, spires and assorted slickrock shapes. Side canyons invite exploration. At 3 miles you start getting up into cooler shaded pine forest and it's a good spot to turn around, stop for lunch and head back.

DIRECTIONS: From the "Y" in Sedona go west on HWY 89A for 3.1 miles to Dry Creek Road. Turn right and go 2 miles to where Dry Creek Road turns right and becomes dirt. The road is rough, but your car will make it if you go slow. The small, well marked parking area is on your left after another 3.4 miles.

STERLING PASS

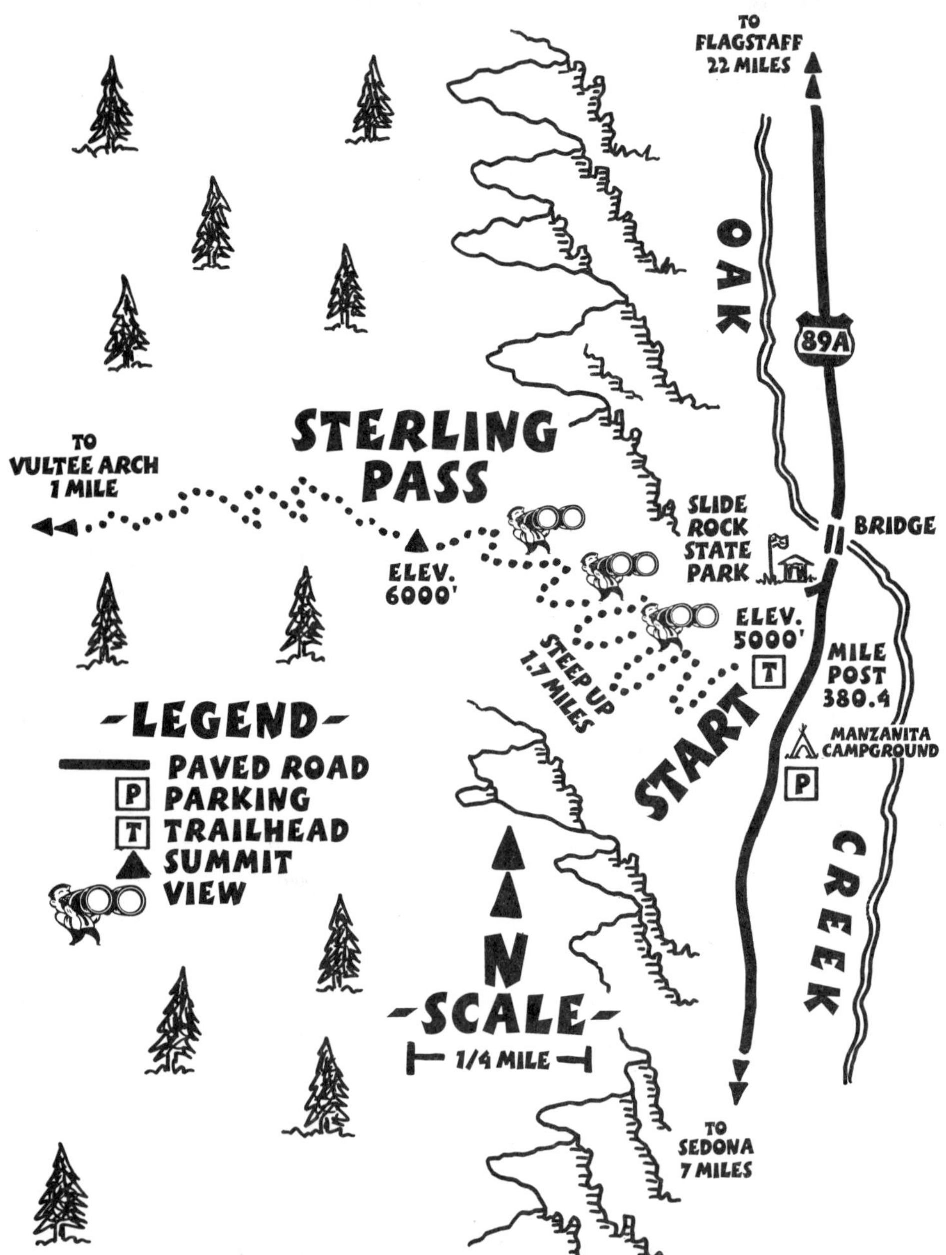

SEDONA

STERLING PASS TRAIL

CLIMB FROM OAK CREEK TO VIEW

DISTANCE: 3.4 MILES
TIME: 1.5 TO 2 HOURS
EFFORT: SHORT & STEEP
TYPE: OUT & BACK
FIND ROUTE: EASY
SEASON: APR to NOV

DESCRIPTION: Leads up and over a high saddle from Oak Creek Canyon to Sterling Canyon. The climb is a steep grunt right from the get-go up a drainage formerly populated with giant, sweet smelling old growth pines. The 2006 Brin's Fire roasted all in its path. The trail has re-opened to a newly exposed view of Oak Creek Canyon's terra cotta and buff sandstone cliffs. Greenery has returned as is nature's way, however, the big trees will take a lifetime to return. Looking to the bright side, we now have opportunity to study the canyon's newly exposed geology.

Although most hikers do a *turn-and-burn* at the top and head back the way they came, I usually continue on a short ways down the other side into Sterling Canyon. Make a short detour to visit Vultee Arch (see Vultee Arch Trail) and meet a support vehicle at the Vultee Arch Trailhead. You'll only add 1.2 downhill miles to your hike *plus* you'll score a bonus visit to Vultee Arch. Promise your couch potato support crew a free lunch in Sedona and they'll most likely be happy to oblige.

DIRECTIONS: From the "Y" in Sedona go 6 miles north on HWY 89A to milepost 380.4 to your trailhead on the left just above Manzanita Campground. Parking is terrible here. There is more available a ways south of Manzanita.

SOLDIER PASS

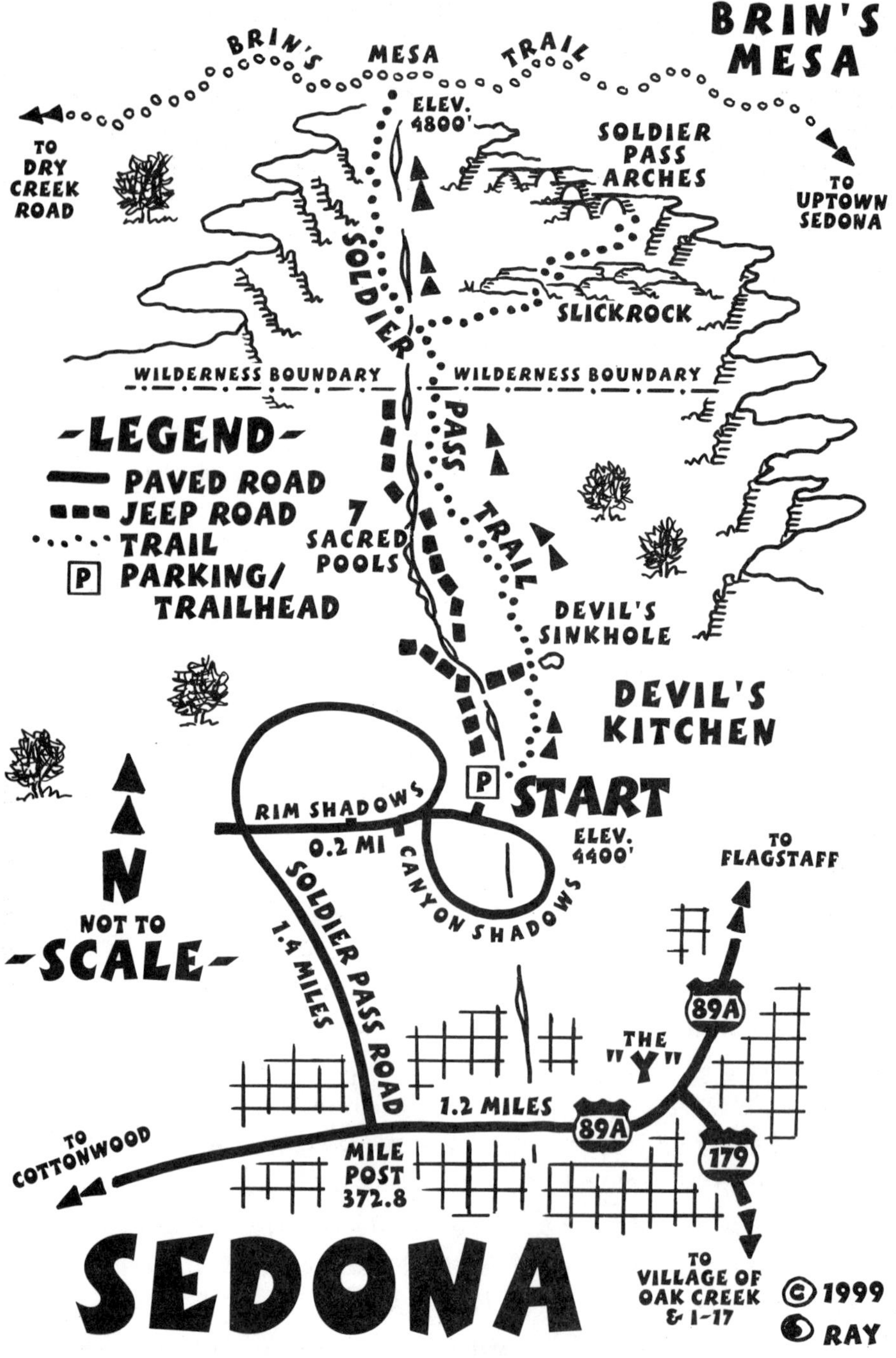

SEDONA

SOLDIER PASS TRAIL
DEVIL'S SINK SECRET ARCHES SEVEN SACRED POOLS

DISTANCE: 2.2 MILES
TIME: 2 HOURS
EFFORT: EASY
TYPE: OUT & BACK
FIND ROUTE: MODERATE
SEASON: ALL YEAR

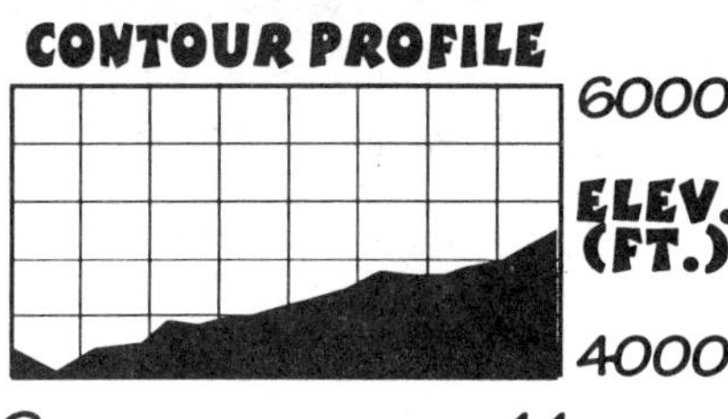

DESCRIPTION: Wow! So much to see so close to town. You are in the shadow of landmark Coffeepot Rock. At the trailhead, look around. Next to Coffeepot find the Native American lookalike redrock formation: Warrior, Woman & Papoose, Young Brave. Due north up Soldier Wash is Soldier Pass, pools and arches.

From the parking lot find the marked trailhead down to the right. Your way is marked with cairns the whole way. Come to Devil's Sinkhole, Sedona's biggest, which opened in the late 1800s. Watch your step!

Continue following cairns and trail to Seven Sacred Pools carved in slickrock, named when this was an only water source and thus sacred. Not good for drinking, but nice for sitting and soaking feet on a hot day. Now again continue to the wilderness boundary and beyond to where the trail splits. Left goes up over Soldier Pass. Right leads up onto a slickrock shelf. Cairns guide you up to the hidden Soldier Pass Arches.

DIRECTIONS: From the "Y" in Sedona go west on 89A for 1.2 miles to Soldier Pass Road. Go right and follow the map to the trailhead parking area. This well heeled neighborhood detests all the tourist traffic, so be cool. But remember, this is *our* national forest.

STEAMBOAT ROCK
(WILSON CANYON)

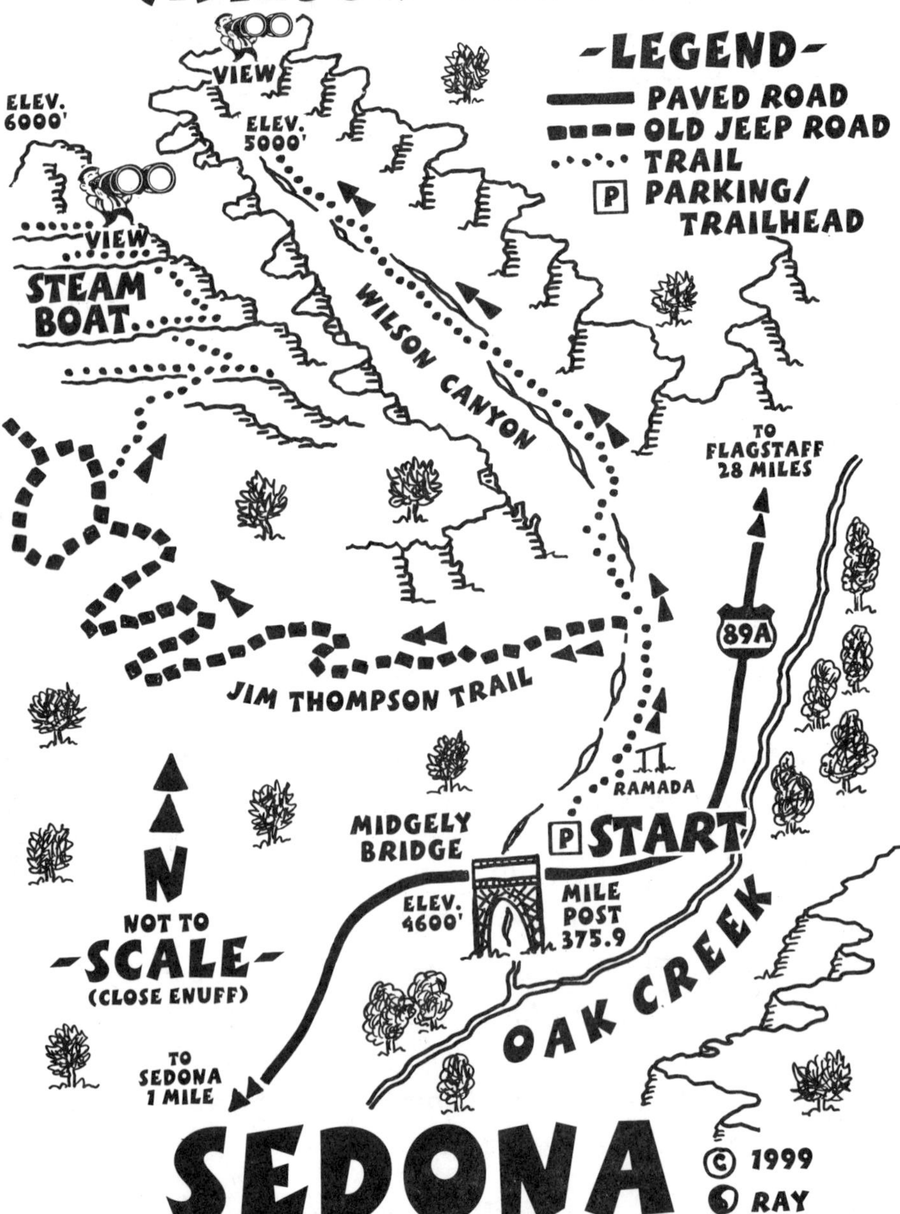

SEDONA

STEAMBOAT ROCK/WILSON CANYON
SCENIC CANYON & POPULAR VIEW

DISTANCE: 3 MILES
TIME: 1.5 TO 2 HOURS
EFFORT: EASY
TYPE: OUT & BACK
FIND ROUTE: EASY
SEASON: ALL YEAR

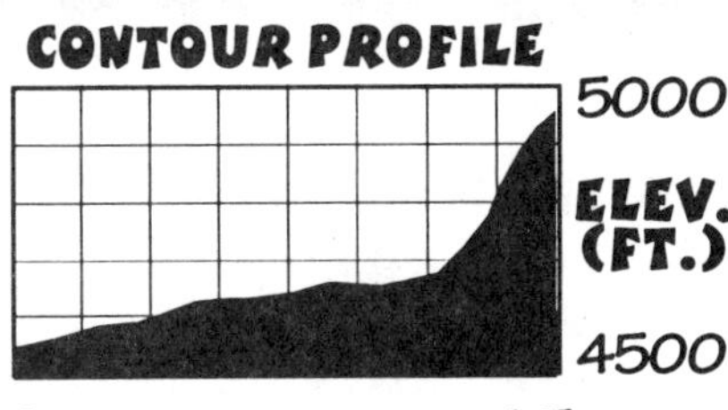

DESCRIPTION: Take a short easy walk up lovely Wilson Canyon or do the wild thing and climb *almost* to the top of Sedona landmark Steamboat Rock.

Richard Wilson died here in a misunderstanding with a bear in 1885. Wilson shot, then came too close to the wounded bear. Died in each other's arms, bless their hearts. No grizzlies now, but Wilson Canyon is still the lovely idyl of 100 years ago. From the signed trailhead it's 1.5 easy, scenic miles to canyon's end where the trail gets steep and you get a view of Wilson and Oak Creek Canyons.

For the *real* view, climb Steamboat Rock. From the trailhead go up Wilson Canyon 0.5 miles to the Jim Thompson Trail sign. LEFT up the old road 0.3 miles to the top where it joins another road. Continue RIGHT another 50 ft. to where a small trail takes off again to the RIGHT up towards Steamboat. WARNING: Tourists die climbing Sedona monuments every year. *Go as high as you dare, but please don't die with this book in hand!*

DIRECTIONS: North from the "Y" in Sedona for 1 mile on HWY 89A to milepost 375.9 at Midgley Bridge and park among the tourist throng. The trailhead sign is by the ramada.

SUBMARINE ROCK
(VIA MORGAN ROAD)

SUBMARINE ROCK
TRAILS EXPLORE SLICKROCK AND VIEWS

DISTANCE: 5 MILES
TIME: 3 TO 4 HOURS
EFFORT: MODERATE
TYPE: OUT & BACK
FIND ROUTE: MODERATE
SEASON: SEP TO MAY

DESCRIPTION: The distances are short, but there are heaps to see in Sedona's slickrock playground. From where the road turns dirt at the end of Morgan Road, avoid the rough jeep road you would share with Pink Jeep Tours. Instead, a trail takes off across the road from the lot. Signs and cairns mark the way.

Be sure and take a quickie side trip to the sinkhole in Devil's Dining Room. Above Devil's Sink is a welter of unmarked trails. It's a whole day's adventure to pick a landmark and head for it. You'll find Battlement Mesa up to the right is a good goal with great views of Sedona. Remember, as with anywhere in Sedona, as long as you keep landmarks in view, you can't get lost. Besides, Pink Jeeps are everywhere.

Now follow the signs to Submarine Rock. Fun to scramble over and explore. Next, follow the map to Slickrock Loop on the other side of the jeep road. Fun to watch Pink Jeep passengers trying to control their panic going down The Stairs. Finish up with a killer view at Chicken Point.

DIRECTIONS: From the "Y" in Sedona go 1.5 miles south on HWY 179 to the "Broken Arrow" sign at Morgan Road. Go LEFT and park in the lot just as the road turns dirt. The trail begins across the road.

SYCAMORE CANYON (PARSONS TRAIL)

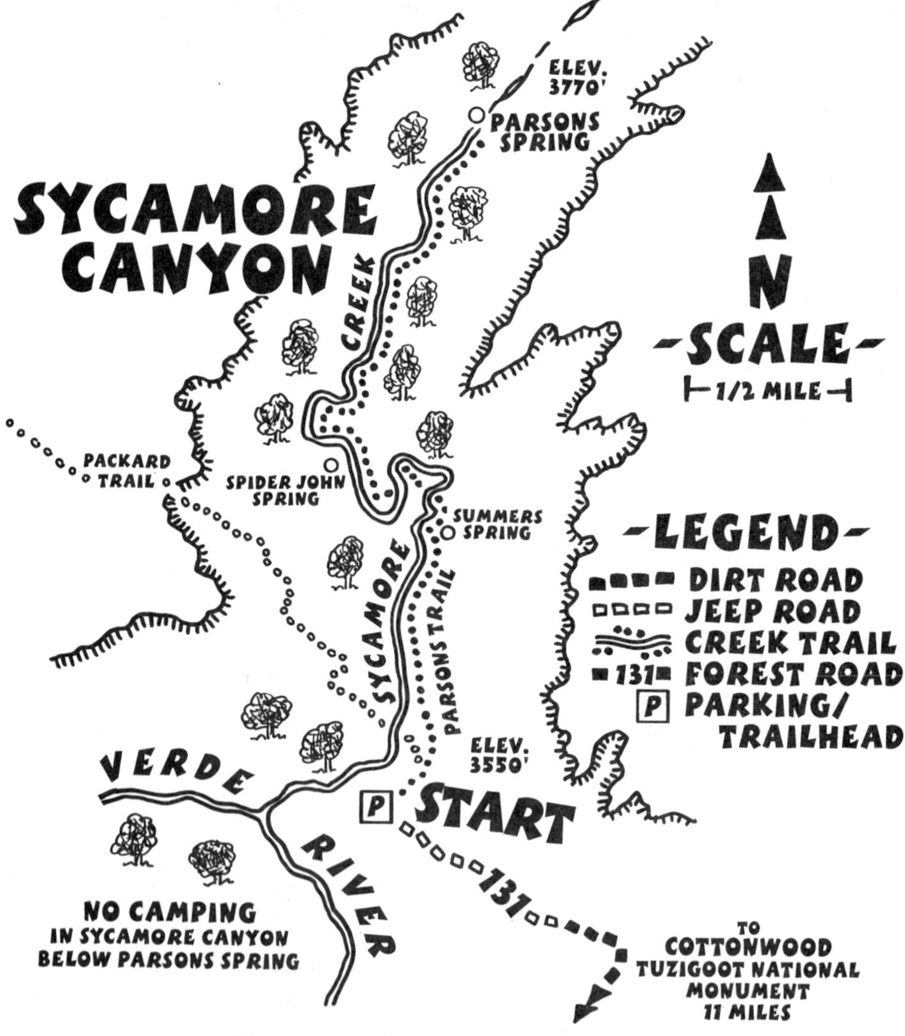

SEDONA (COTTONWOOD)

SYCAMORE CREEK
SHADED TRAIL UP A BEAUTIFUL CREEK

DISTANCE: 8 MILES
TIME: 4 TO 5 HOURS
EFFORT: MODERATE
TYPE: OUT & BACK
FIND ROUTE: CAN BE A LITTLE TRICKY
SEASON: SEP TO JUNE

DESCRIPTION: Sycamore Creek rolls out of the Sycamore Canyon Wilderness west of Sedona and pretty much defines the world of riparian wildlife habitat in Northern Arizona. There is nothing quite so fine to man, bird or beast as water in the desert. Parsons Trail allows for some very most excellent exploration of the lower end of Sycamore Canyon.

The trailhead is just above where Sycamore Creek meets the Verde River. The trail drops down a couple of hundred feet to the creek right at the start and then continues upstream for 4 miles to Parsons Spring. The trail makes several creek crossings and may not be do-able during spring runoff. Also, trail damage from a recent flood has yet to be repaired. If you lose the trail, follow the creek and wear your Tevas or tennies for this creek style hike.

There are cattle nearby. That means giardia. This water is *NOT* safe to drink. Do not drink *ANY* creek or spring water along the way. Same goes for your pets. Camping is not allowed below Parsons Spring.

DIRECTIONS: Easy to find. From the "Y" in Sedona, go 20 miles southwest on HWY 89A to Cottonwood. Continue through Cottonwood on Main Street then Broadway until you turn RIGHT at the sign for Tuzigoot National Monument. Cross a bridge over the Verde River then take FS 131, the first dirt road on your LEFT, for 11 miles as it *mostly* follows The Verde to the trailhead parking area.

VULTEE ARCH

VULTEE ARCH
ELEV. 5500'
STERLING PASS
START
ELEV. 5000'
N
NOT TO
-SCALE-
152
4.4 MILES
DRY CREEK ROAD
TO BOYNTON PASS
-LEGEND-
PAVED ROAD
BUMPY DIRT ROAD
TRAIL
FOREST ROAD
P PARKING/ TRAILHEAD
TO FLAGSTAFF
2.0 MILES
89A
THE "Y"
89A
179
TO COTTONWOOD
MILE POST 371
3.1 MILES
TO VILLAGE OF OAK CREEK & I-17
SEDONA
© 1999 RAY

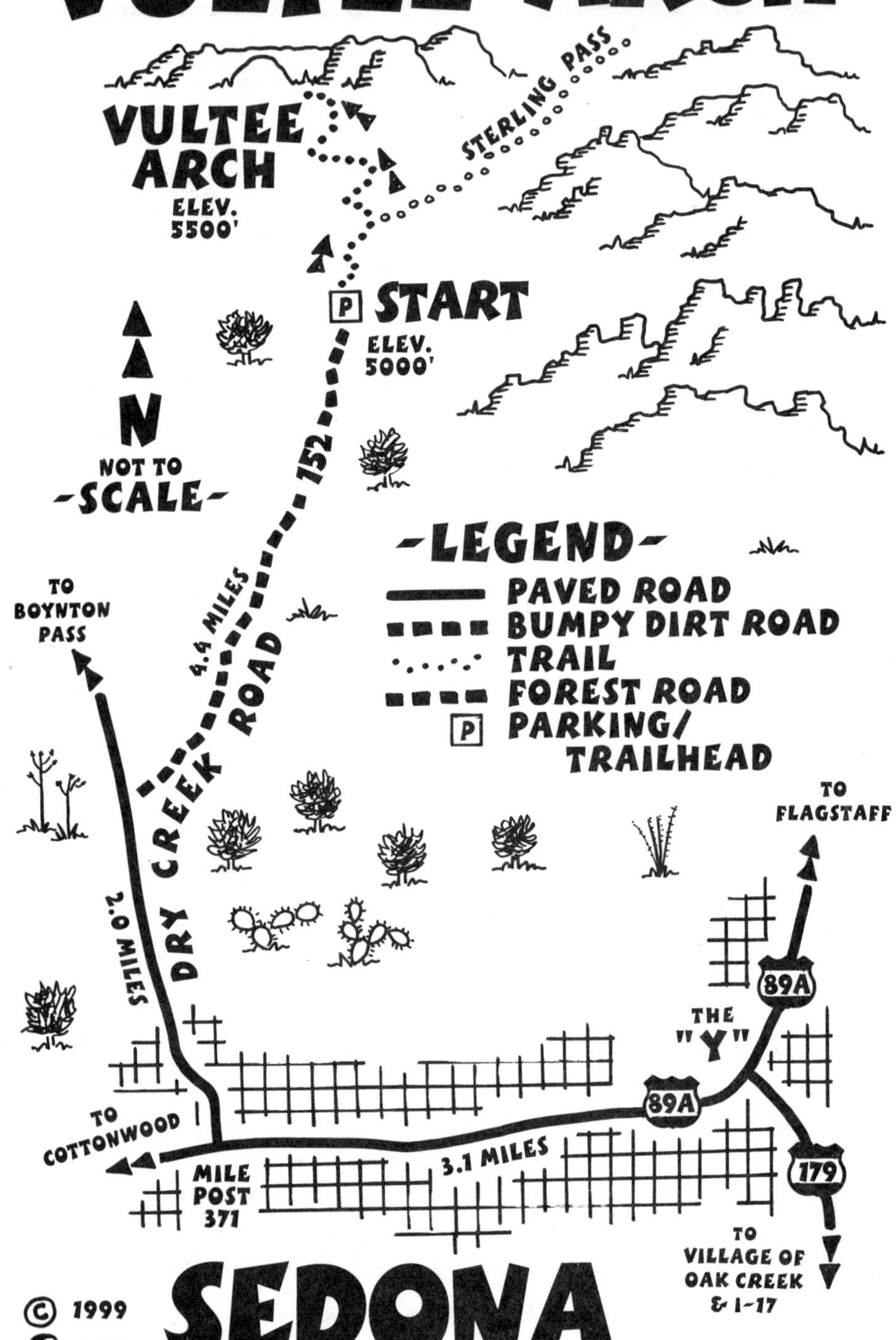

VULTEE ARCH

EASY STROLL TO SEDONA'S FAVORITE ARCH

DISTANCE: 3.2 MILES
TIME: 2 HOURS
EFFORT: EASY
TYPE: OUT & BACK
FIND ROUTE: EASY
SEASON: ALL YEAR

DESCRIPTION: January 9, 1938, aircraft designer Gerald Vultee and wife Sylvia augered their plane into East Pocket Mesa just above here after engine trouble in a snowstorm. This terra cotta arch on the north wall of Sterling Canyon was named for them as a plaque attests. Vultee Arch Trail is an easy smooth hike in scenic Sterling Canyon to this sensational sandstone arch. No wonder so darn many Sedona feet beat a path to Vultee Arch. It's got history. It's gorgeous. It's a groovy spot.

Vultee Arch is 40' high and 50' long. Those with nerve and no sense of vertigo can climb up to and out upon if they so desire. Vultee appears to be darn solid so there be no risk of collapse. However, although it's plenty wide, falling off the arch is *always* a possibility.

The only real problem you may encounter at Vultee is on the way out on car thrasher road FS152. Taken at speed you will feel like a pip in a rattle. Your car will hate you. Unless you are drive a rental and don't give a flying phooey, you should take it easy. Thousands of cars make it no prob and you can too. Just go slow.

DIRECTIONS: From the "Y" in Sedona go west on HWY 89A for 3.1 miles to paved Dry Creek Road at milepost 371. Turn right and go 2 miles to semi-rough dirt FS152 and turn right. Go 4.5 miles to the end of the road and park in the lot.

WEST FORK OF OAK CREEK

SEDONA

WEST FORK TRAIL
SPLASH UP A SCENIC CANYON CREEK

DISTANCE: 6 MILES
TIME: 2 TO 3 HOURS
EFFORT: EASY
TYPE: OUT & BACK
FIND ROUTE: EASY
SEASON: MAR to NOV

DESCRIPTION: The idyllic little stream that is the West Fork of Oak Creek snakes down out of Secret Mountain Wilderness through sculptured Coconino sandstone canyon cliffs 1000 ft. high.

In spring, songbirds trill and dot the trees with flashes of color. Summer gives cool respite from Arizona's ovens. And fall is the magic time. Red and gold leaf pastels of maple and oak drift like tiny boats along a string of mirrored pools connected by a softly splashing brook. No wonder West Fork is most visited trail in Coconino National Forest.

The marked path wanders three easy out and back miles upstream under views of towering terra cotta cliffs. Wear tennies or TEVAs as West Fork Trail zig-zags across the creek on stepping stones and quick splashes in shallow water. If you continue upstream for more of the creek's entire 14 mile length to where it begins near Woody Mountain Road west of Flagstaff, be ready for lots of stream bed wading, boulder hopping and swimming.

DIRECTIONS: *Go* 10 miles north of Sedona or 19 miles south of Flagstaff on HWY 89A to milepost 384.5. You can't miss it. The forest service has built a huge new parking area with fancy stonework poopers and a nice bridge across Oak Creek. Pay to park or park for free in a wide spot up the highway.

WILSON MTN NORTH

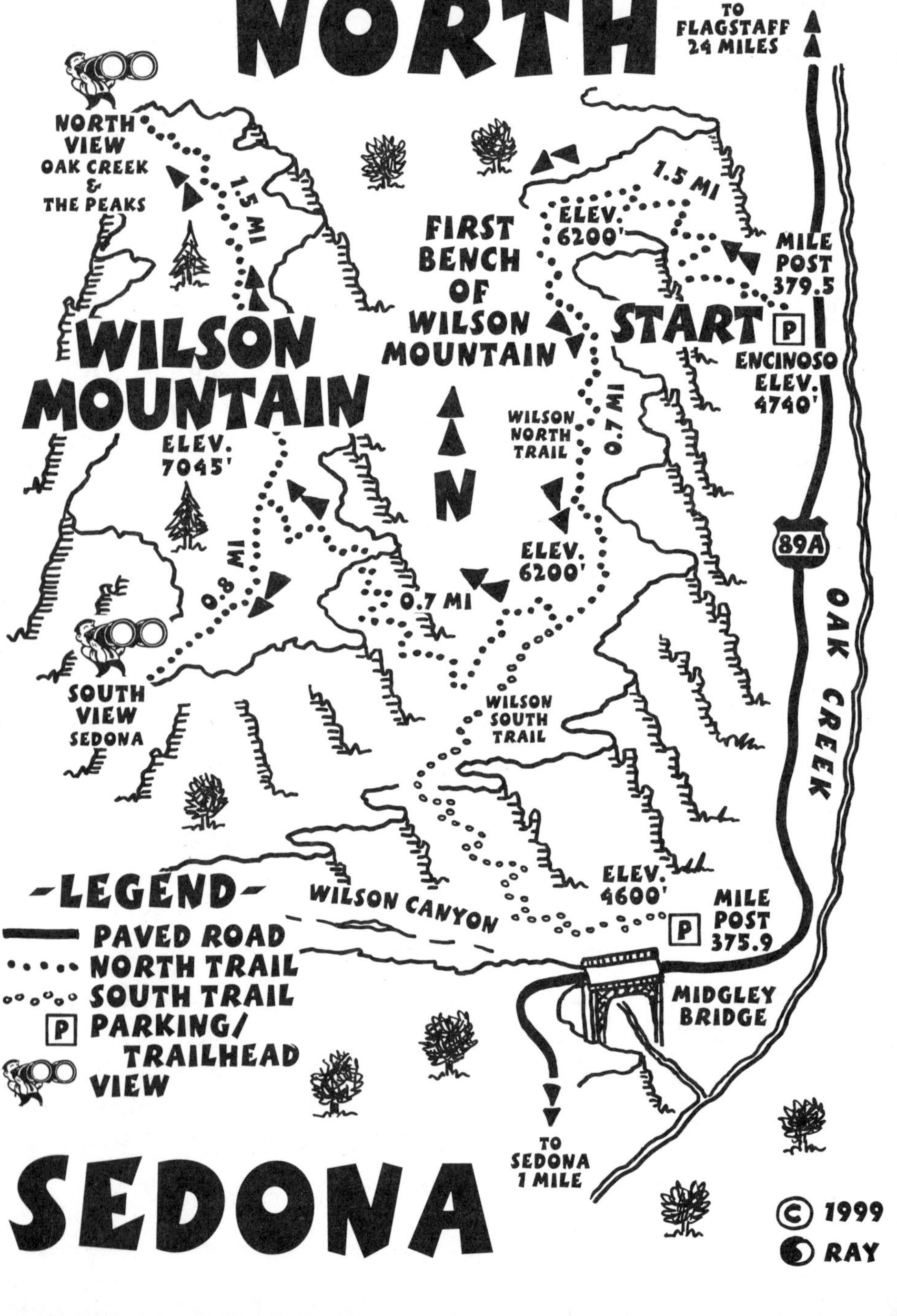

TO FLAGSTAFF 24 MILES

NORTH VIEW OAK CREEK & THE PEAKS

1.5 MI

WILSON MOUNTAIN

ELEV. 7045'

0.8 MI

SOUTH VIEW SEDONA

FIRST BENCH OF WILSON MOUNTAIN

N

0.7 MI

ELEV. 6200'

1.5 MI

ELEV. 6200'

WILSON NORTH TRAIL

0.7 MI

START

MILE POST 379.5

P

ENCINOSO ELEV. 4740'

89A

OAK CREEK

WILSON SOUTH TRAIL

ELEV. 4600'

MILE POST 375.9

P

WILSON CANYON

MIDGLEY BRIDGE

TO SEDONA 1 MILE

-LEGEND-

PAVED ROAD

NORTH TRAIL

SOUTH TRAIL

P PARKING/ TRAILHEAD

VIEW

SEDONA

WILSON MOUNTAIN NORTH
TOUGH CLIMB TO GREAT VIEWS

DISTANCE: 7.4 MILES
TIME: 5 TO 6 HOURS
EFFORT: STEEP UP
TYPE: OUT & BACK
FIND ROUTE: EASY
SEASON: APR TO NOV

CONTOUR PROFILE

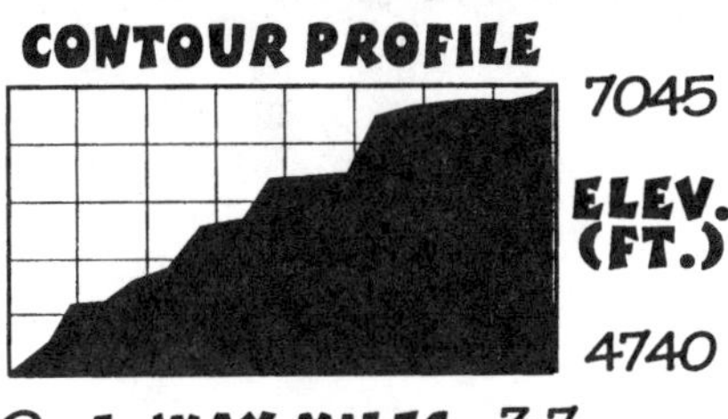

DESCRIPTION: The top of Wilson Mountain, directly overhead north of Sedona, boasts two of the most eyeball poppin' views in AZ. The 2006 Brin's Fire had closed the trail for a time, but has now re-opened. Wilson is a 3000' double-decker red stone mesa. The broad lower mesa, named First Bench of Wilson, forms a base for the mountain's slightly smaller top mesa.

The view from the summit's south end is like being in an airplane 3000' above Sedona. Bring binoculars. Then walk 2.3 miles to the narrow mesa's north end and WOW! A direct view up Oak Creek with a telephoto shot of The San Francisco Peaks popping straight up out of Oak Creek Canyon. In late fall, when The Canyon turns red and gold and The Peaks are first cloaked in a white mantle, you'll stare all agog as you eat your lunch.

Wilson Mountain trails have re-opened, but due to debris and erosion there is still some slight danger. Crews have cleared the trail and replanted. Nature is taking its course and life returns. The mountain is already showing signs of new life and the freshly exposed views are better than ever.

DIRECTIONS: Go 4.6 miles north of Sedona on HWY 89A to Encinoso Picnic Area at milepost 379.5 and park. The marked trailhead is just north a few steps.

WILSON MTN SOUTH
TO FLAGSTAFF 24 MILES
NORTH VIEW OAK CREEK & THE PEAKS
1.5 MI
ELEV. 6200'
FIRST BENCH OF WILSON MOUNTAIN
MILE POST 379.5
P
ELEV. 4740'
WILSON MOUNTAIN
ELEV. 7045'
N
WILSON NORTH TRAIL
89A
OAK CREEK
ELEV. 6200'
0.8 MI
0.7 MI
SOUTH VIEW SEDONA
WILSON SOUTH TRAIL
START
1.5 MI
WILSON CANYON
P
ELEV. 4600'
MILE POST 375.9
-LEGEND-
PAVED ROAD
NORTH TRAIL
SOUTH TRAIL
P PARKING/ TRAILHEAD
VIEW
TO SEDONA 1 MILE

SEDONA

WILSON MOUNTAIN SOUTH
TOUGH SUNNY CLIMB TO PANORAMAS

DISTANCE: 5.8 MILES
TIME: 4 TO 5 HOURS
EFFORT: STEEP UP
TYPE: OUT & BACK
FIND ROUTE: EASY
SEASON: APR to NOV

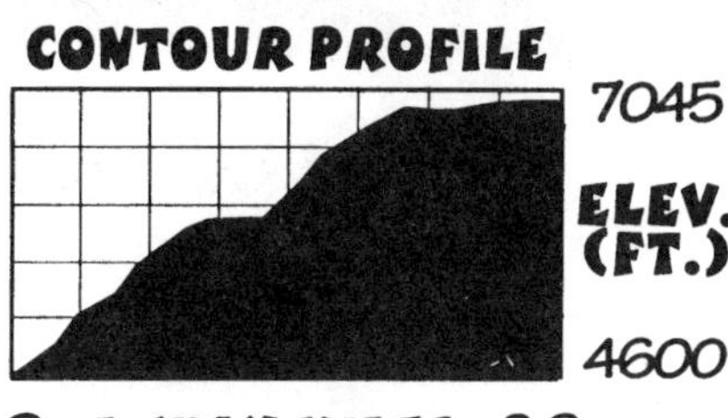

DESCRIPTION: The Brin's Fire sparked up from an illegal and unattended campfire June 18, 2006 and was not contained until June 27. Over 4,000 acres were burned. This was Sedona's premiere "view hike" and, take heart, is again as it re-opened in 2008. Many tears were shed at the time of the fire, but life has returned, many more new views have been exposed and time will heal all that was lost.

Wilson South ascends lofty heights via a route suited to the cooler months as it first climbs the warm and sunny south face of the mountain before joining Wilson North for the last grunt to the top.

Wilson South is frequently done in winter when the 7000' flat top often has no snow and the way up is dry. However, Wilson South is usually too hot in summer. That's when the canyon climb up Wilson North is best. In any event, it's no small achievement for many just to make it up to First Bench.

BEGIN at the Midgely Bridge parking area. Head for the picnic ramada. There a sign points you the RIGHT direction . . . UP! The first pitch is steep and rough all the way to First Bench until the trail connects with Wilson North Trail. Pack lots of water, binoculars, snack and a hat.

DIRECTIONS: North from Sedona on HWY 89A for 1 mile to Midgely Bridge and park.

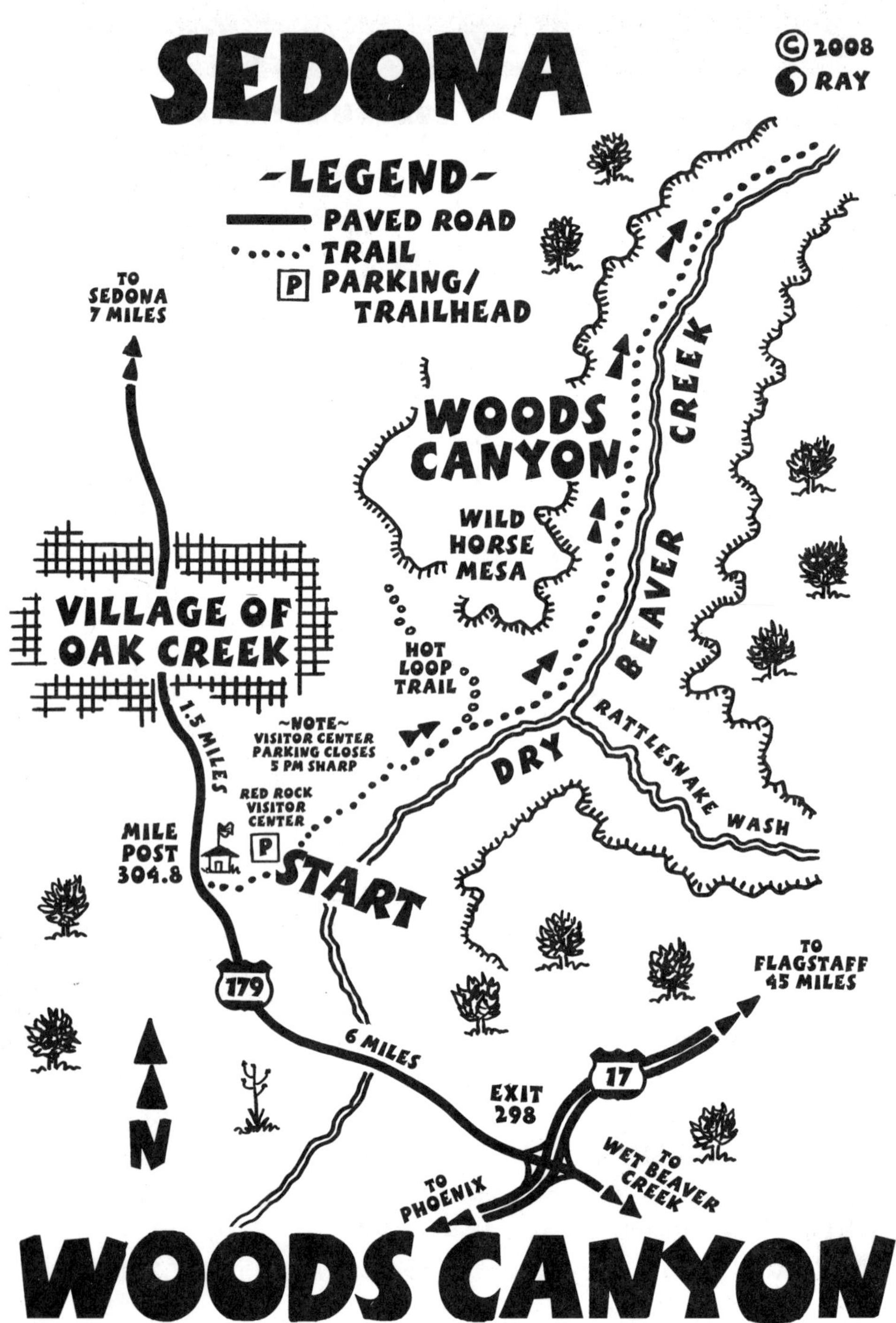

WOODS CANYON

WOODS CANYON

SPRINGTIME MEANS BIG WATER

DISTANCE: 6 TO 10 MILES
TIME: 3 TO 5 HOURS
EFFORT: MODERATE
TYPE: OUT & BACK
FIND ROUTE: EASY
SEASON: OCT TO MAY

DESCRIPTION: This stellar hike up a wild, remote canyon 9 miles south of Sedona is best done in the spring when snowmelt from the forests above Woods Canyon feed Dry Beaver Creek to a fury. The trail winds above the creekbed with no crossings. I've seen deer, beaver, javelina and a fresh set of bear tracks plus many, many birds. This trail is an out and back only because the upper portion of 12 mile long Woods is very gnarly and only ultra hard core types would be able to do its full length. However, the first 5 miles are enjoyable for most anyone as you get into really glorious country. Hike up the canyon until you are about half pooped out, saving your other half for the return. In summer, it's hot and Dry Beaver reverts to nearly dry puddles and pools.

START at the brand new Red Rock Visitor Center 9 miles south of Sedona (1.5 miles south of The Village of Oak Creek) at milepost 304.8 on HWY 179.

WARNING . . . there is no formal trailhead nor actual trailhead parking lot as of this writing. You may park in the visitor center parking lot, but the lot closes and is LOCKED after 5 PM sharp. A new trailhead and parking area will be located just south of the Visitor Center in the near future.

DIRECTIONS: The Red Rock Visitor Center at Milepost 304.8 on HWY 179 is located 6 miles north of I-17, 1.5 miles south of Village of Oak Creek and and 9 miles south of Sedona.

BACKTALK

Hi, I'm Cosmic Ray and despite the name I am a real person. In small towns like Flag and Sedona people are often applied a handle to distinguish them from others of the same name. No kidding, I was really given this by friends and it stuck. Why Cosmic? Why not? Good as any, I reckon.

My maps are adapted from topos and forest service charts. They are oriented north and as close to scale as I can make them and still fit on a page. I like to think they have a human look rather than being drawn with a mouse and computer. I've been told they look more like notes from a buddy than a handbook. I like that because it's true. I hope you have as much fun with this guide as I had creating it.

Humble thanks to my many fine friends who helped with ideas, advice and sweat. Muchas gracias to pals Eric and Jane for cover and inside art. Special thanks to wife Marcia and *Cosmic Dirt Squirt* Elena Marie who add love and understanding. With friends and family, we can wander forever and never be lost. Wherever you go, there you are!

13th (GULP!) *EDITION*

COSMIC RAY

3960 N. Zurich St. Flagstaff, AZ 86004

FAX: (928) 526-8243

e-mail: cozray@juno.com